Our Debt to Greece and Rome

EDITORS
GEORGE DEPUE HADZSITS, PH.D.

DAVID MOORE ROBINSON, PH.D., LL.D.

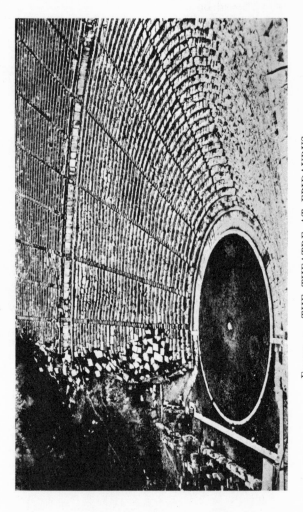

FIGURE 1. THE THEATRE AT EPIDAURUS

From a photograph by Dr. C. W. Blegen

STAGE ANTIQUITIES OF THE GREEKS AND ROMANS AND THEIR INFLUENCE

BY

JAMES TURNEY ALLEN, Ph.D.

COOPER SQUARE PUBLISHERS, INC.

NEW YORK

1963

PA
3201
.A6
1963

Published 1963 by Cooper Square Publishers, Inc.
59 Fourth Avenue, New York 3, N. Y.
Library of Congress Catalog Card No. 63-10266

PREFACE

THE SUBJECT of this volume appears at first sight to be tripartite. In fact, however, it is essentially bipartite, and the title might well have been " The Stage Antiquities of the Greeks and Their Influence." For among the ancient Romans the theatre and the dramatic art in its several aspects were very largely importations from various parts of the Hellenic world. In the following pages, therefore, the subject of influence is not confined to chapters XI and XII, as one might at first suppose, but chapters II and IV and parts of VI, VII, VIII, IX, and X belong here as well.

The limitations of space have made necessary a rigorous selection of material and a high degree of condensation. In consequence many details have had to be sacrificed, even whole topics omitted. Controversial matters especially have been pruned to the quick. The result, I fear, will please no one, even as it fails to satisfy my own desires. But if it shall appear that the most essential facts have been presented and that in a reasonably clear and unbiassed manner, I shall rest content. One aspect of the subject in particular, although not wholly neglected, could not be presented with the fullness that it deserves: the relation of the physical playhouse and the mechanics of stagecraft to dramatic literature and the art of the theatre. Yet herein lies the real justification of a study of stage antiquities.

The completion of this book was delayed by reason of a sojourn of eight months in Greece. But the delay I neither regret nor deplore. Rather the opportunity to study the ancient theatres at first hand and especially to examine with minute care over and over again every detail of the great Dionysiac theatre at Athens was a priceless privilege, and for this privilege I wish to acknowledge my debt of gratitude to the Managing Committee of the American School of Classical Studies at Athens and to the President and Regents of the University of California. I desire also to thank Professor Lily B. Campbell of the University of California, Southern Branch, Los Angeles, for generously loaning me her copy of Conte Montenari's *Del Teatro Olimpico,* 1749, a book that is very difficult to obtain; and the editors of this Series for their courteous patience and for numerous most helpful suggestions.

BERKELEY, CALIFORNIA.
December 20, 1926

CONTENTS

[ix]

CONTENTS

ILLUSTRATIONS

[xi]

ILLUSTRATIONS

STAGE ANTIQUITIES OF THE GREEKS AND ROMANS AND THEIR INFLUENCE

STAGE ANTIQUITIES
OF THE
GREEKS AND ROMANS

I. GREEK DRAMA

> Sometime let gorgeous **Tragedy**
> In sceptered pall come sweeping by
> Presenting Thebes or Pelops' line
> Or the tale of Troy divine.[1]

IN SPITE of earthquake and the wanton
deeds of war the Parthenon is still one of
the most impressive of all buildings. Though
old, it is ever young; though shaken and bat-
tered, ever fresh. Even in its ruins it is glorious.
And yet if one would understand its significance
as a work of art, if one would have more than a
merely superficial appreciation even of its
beauty, there is necessary some acquaintance
with the progress of sculpture and architecture
from crude idol and archaic shrine until there
was rendered possible the conception and the
creation of this majestic temple. Greek drama
affords a close parallel. Its masterpieces belong
to the same period as the Parthenon, and though

old, they too are ever young, for theirs is the un-
fading freshness of immortal youth. They too
can be adequately understood only if we see in
them the sublimation of centuries of poetic development, and if we acquaint ourselves as best
we may with their various component elements
and the processes by which these elements were
combined and fused into the perfect product.

Three forms of drama were created and ele-
vated to the rank of literature by the Greeks:
tragedy, comedy, and a unique type known as
satyr-play or satyr-drama, the name of which
should not be confused with ' satire,' ' satirical,'
nor yet with the Latin ' satura ' (p. 21). The
origin of each of these several species of dramatic composition presents a problem of baffling
difficulty. Certain facts, indeed, are clear and
accepted by all; others are shrouded in a veil
of obscurity from which they may never be
disengaged.

For hundreds of years prior to the creation
of the drama the Greeks had cultivated melic
poetry, that is poetry intended to be sung to
instrumental accompaniment, and in its choral
form to the accompaniment also of graceful and
expressive dance movements, and this without
doubt was the source from which were derived

[4]

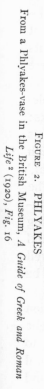

FIGURE 2. PHLYAKES

From a Phlyakes-vase in the British Museum, *A Guide of Greek and Roman Life* [2] (1920), *Fig.* 16

the majestic choral odes of tragedy as also its solos and lyrical dialogues. Gifts of the melic poets too were the lyric portions of satyr-play and of comedy. Other features were contributed by the earlier art of the epic, such as subjects and plots, setting, atmosphere, even certain elements of style and technique. The *Iliad* and the *Odyssey* of Homer, the various poems of the Epic Cycle, the *Homeric Hymns,* the works of Hesiod, and the productions of similar kinds, constituted a well-filled store-house from which drama, especially tragedy and satyr-play, drew with lavish hand. During the seventh and sixth centuries other types of poetic composition also, poems in iambic and trochaic verse-forms, were perfected and widely cultivated. These too contributed richly to the growth of the drama.

But no one of these literary forms of itself, nor all of them together were sufficient to bring drama into being. They but formed, as it were, an environment by which the character of drama, once started on its course, was in a measure determined. The life-giving germ was found rather in rude performances engaged in by the common folk of countryside and village in connection with various religious festivals

and rites. The essence of dramatic art is mime-
sis, representation, impersonation. The mimetic
element in these primitive entertainments and
revels, the act of losing one's own identity for
the nonce and merging it imaginatively in the
personality of another — this it was that provided the generative impulse.

Out of performances of this sort there developed rude plays of various types, which went
by different names in different localities. Such
mimes or farces flourished in Dorian communities of the Peloponnesus, Sicily, and Southern
Italy, but seldom rose to the dignity of literature. In Sicily, however, Epicharmus of Syracuse (c. 475 B.C.) and one or two others wrought
out of these lowly materials simple dramas of
literary form, of which a few fragments have
been preserved. They were in part mythological
travesties, in part amusing scenes depicting the
common incidents of everyday life. Two hundred years later a certain Rhinthon of Tarentum in Southern Italy is said to have aspired to
literary fame by the writing of burlesque paro-
dies of tragedies based upon myths of gods and
heroes. His plays have been lost, but like the
comedies of Epicharmus they too were rooted
in the Dorian mime. The performers of such

mimes were known in the Greek settlements of Italy as *phlyakes*. The burlesque shows which they presented were not without influence upon Plautine comedy and scenes from them were favorite subjects with the vase painters of Magna Graecia (fig. 2). Of great antiquity, the mime continued to flourish during the golden age of the drama and ultimately, as we shall see, took almost complete possession of the stage (p. 25).

Another form of masquerade was known as the *comus* (κῶμος) and was very popular in Attica. From the name, which designated not only the revel but the band of revelers as well, was derived the word comedy (κωμῳδία), that is 'revel-song' (ᾠδή, song). The comus, like the primitive mummery which gave rise to Dorian farce, was perhaps in origin a phallic ceremony, a rite of sexual magic. The performers dressed in amusing costumes representing birds, cocks, horses, dolphins, and the like, danced and sang and indulged in ritualistic scurrility and obscene ribaldry. Often the band would form a procession and with a huge phallic symbol borne on a pole would march from house to house to the music of a clarinet [2] and render a program of singing and dancing combined

[7]

with scurrilous jokes. All was extemporaneous in character.

In time the custom arose of holding comuses in an orchestra (p. 61). If records may be trusted and are correctly interpreted, this innovation was introduced by a certain Susarion at Icaria, a village of Attica on the northern slope of Pentelicus not far from the plain of Marathon, and a centre of Dionysiac worship. Early in the sixth century sometime between the years 580 and 560 B.C., these semi-dramatic choral performances were brought, we are told,[3] to Athens and became a regular feature of the old Lenaean festival (p. 32). Later, about 501 B.C., they were added also to the City Dionysia (p. 34). Many believe that the combination of comus-chorus and the clowns of the Dorian farce gave rise to Attic comedy. Exactly when this step was taken, if indeed it was actually taken, is not known, nor under whose leadership. The early history of comedy is very obscure, and it was not until as late as 486 B.C. that comedy received official recognition at Athens and came under the supervision of the state.[4]

Thus it was at the two annual celebrations, the Lenaea and the City Dionysia, and under the influence of tragedy which was already well advanced on the road to perfection, that Athenian comedy came to maturity. The first form to be developed was Old Comedy, the comedy of the fifth century B.C., best known to us through extant plays of Aristophanes (446?–385 B.C.). This was an exuberant, choral and dramatic extravaganza in which satire and burlesque accompanied by fierce political and personal invective and acting of the slap-stick variety predominated. Complex in structure and wholly local in color and theme, its course was quickly run. It did not survive the downfall of Athens at the close of the disastrous Peloponnesian War (404 B.C.). About three quarters of a century later, that is about 330 B.C., arose a new type, more refined and less local in color known as New Comedy. This was a comedy of manners best illustrated by the extensive fragments of Menander (343–291 B.C.), the plays of Plautus and Terence, and such modern adaptations as Molière's *Amphitruo* and *L'Avare* and Shakespeare's *Comedy of Errors*. A third form, sometimes designated Middle Comedy, was merely a transitional stage between these two. It flourished for about three-quarters of a century from the decline of Old Comedy after the close of the fifth century to the rise of New Comedy in the days of Alexander the Great, with a certain amount of overlapping at either end. This so-called Middle Comedy, less satirical than the Old and lacking both its exuberant spirit and metrical variety, delighted in the parody of tragedy and of other species of serious literature and in the piquant portrayal of certain types familiar in contemporary Athenian society.[5]

From this brief account of the rise and development of comedy let us turn back to consider satyr-drama and tragedy. One of the sources of the former, as probably also of the latter, is found in certain phallic mummeries, in which the performers imagined themselves to represent nature-sprites, vegetation spirits which were supposed to resemble animals, horses or goats, and were popularly known as *sileni* or *satyri* (satyrs). Dressed in the semblance of such creatures, the performers engaged in grotesque dances at religious festivals, some in the service of Dionysus, others as attendants upon Pan or other gods of field and woodland. From the union of such uncouth rustic revelries with a hymn, which went by the name of dithyramb, there was born with the maieutic aid of a certain Pratinas of Phlius the curious type of play known as satyr-drama.[6] In a sense this was a hybrid type as it consisted in part of constant stock characters, in part of variant or free characters. The stock characters were the chorus of satyrs, and an actor who impersonated a Silenus and who by a fiction not altogether clear was supposed to be the father of the satyrs. Coarse and bestial were the features of Silenus and shaggy his tight-fitting costume (fig. 3; he stands to the right of Heracles in the upper row), while the make-up of the choreutae comprised loin-bands of cloth or skin, each with phallic symbol and tail attached, and masks with animal ears (fig. 3). The choice of the other characters in the play was determined by the exigencies of the plot: Costumes would vary with the choice, and might on occasion resemble even those common in tragedy, as is shown in figure 3 (the two actors standing nearest the centre in the upper row). Indeed tragedy exercised a considerable influence upon this species of drama, though the tone was far from tragic. The subject was regularly some humorous story taken from mythology or legend and it was treated in a vein of sportive and even obscene gaiety. The best example is

the *Cyclops* of Euripides, in which the " variant " characters are Odysseus and his followers
(the latter as mutes) and the one-eyed giant
Polyphemus.[7]

The origin of satyr-drama, though complex,
is fairly clear. Tragedy presents a problem far
more difficult. Indeed, there is hardly an item
in the early history of Greek tragedy that is not
the subject of controversy so that to chart a
satisfactory course between the Charybdis of
tradition and the many-headed Scylla of modern theory is well-nigh impossible. Throughout
the greater portion of the nineteenth century
the view prevailed that tragedy was but satyr-
drama refined of its dross and raised by the
addition of extraneous elements to a plane of
majestic beauty. In other words, tragedy was
thought to be the child of the satyr-play. Today
the tendency is rather to hold that the two were
separate in origin, or at most related as sister
arts.

This last view we may adopt as on the whole
most plausible. Like satyr-drama, tragedy is
said to have been an off-shoot of the dithyramb as cultivated at Corinth by Arion. Aristotle states definitely that tragedy " was improvisational in origin and derived from the leaders

of the dithyramb." [8] But it is probably wrong
to ascribe a single origin to a work of art so
complex. The early poets who devoted themselves to the task of perfecting this new art-
form borrowed freely, as we have seen, from
epic, melic, and iambo-trochaic poetry. There
is little doubt too that rites at the tomb of a
local hero, the rituals of the mysteries, even
sympathetic magic were drawn upon to make
the final product more artistic and impressive. [9]

The word tragedy ($\tau\rho\alpha\gamma\omega\delta\acute{\iota}\alpha$) apparently
means goat-song ($\tau\rho\acute{\alpha}\gamma os$, goat; $\acute{\omega}\delta\acute{\eta}$, song),
but why this name was adopted remains a lit-
erary and philological puzzle. Some scholars
see in it a reference to the costume worn by the
satyrs in Arion's dithyrambic performances.
Others hold that it arose from the custom of
giving in early days a goat as a prize to the
victorious poet. Others again ascribe it to the
sacrifice of a goat in connection with the ritual.
Indeed, more than a dozen different explana-
tions have been proposed. [10] Be the truth in the
matter as it may, the name $\tau\rho\alpha\gamma\omega\delta\acute{\iota}\alpha$ became
current apparently very early. There came into
use also the word $\tau\rho\alpha\gamma\omega\delta o\acute{\iota}$, ' goat-singers ' or
singers of the ' goat-song,' a term employed to
signify sometimes ' tragic performance,' some-

times 'tragic troupe,' and, in the singular (τραγῳδός) as well as the plural, even 'tragic poet,' 'tragic actor,' and the like. It corresponded roughly to our word tragedian.

Whatever the reason for the adoption of the name, and whatever the precise process by which the various component elements were selected and merged and the earlier satyric tone replaced by one of seriousness and dignity, it was reserved for Attica and Athens to bring tragedy to the full flower of perfected art. The earliest name here is that of Thespis, who lived in the sixth century B.C. in the village of Icaria (p. 8). The step taken by this obscure poet is said to have been the introduction of an actor who addressed the chorus, engaged in dialogue with their leader, and by changes of costume and mask impersonated different characters. Thespian drama was probably crude. Its choreutae and choral songs may have resembled those of the satyr-play. On this point opinion is divided. But practically all are agreed that by the addition of an extra performer in the rôle of actor Thespis completed the foundations of Greek dramatic art.[11] Thereafter the task of raising the superstructure proceeded rapidly, a labor in which many shared. But the

[14]

two who contributed most to the perfecting of
the new art, who gave it strength and exalted
dignity and majestic beauty, were Aeschylus
and Sophocles. Aeschylus (525–456 B.C.) added
a second actor and made many improvements
of far-reaching consequence both in substance
and form, as well as in such externals as costume
and setting. Sophocles (497–406/5 B.C.) added
a third actor and thereby made possible more
searching portrayal of character and greater
complexity of plot-construction. Euripides
(485?–406 B.C.), the third and last great tragic
poet of Athens, was inferior in some respects
to the other two, but did more than they to uni-
versalize dramatic art. It was not an accident
that for hundreds of years following the fifth
century Euripides alone of the tragic poets enjoyed a vogue that was coextensive with Greek
civilization.

Shortly after the death of Euripides and
Sophocles Athens suffered a humiliating defeat
at the hands of her enemies (404 B.C.) and
therewith the golden age of Athenian tragedy
came to an end. During the fourth and third
centuries tragedies continued to be produced in
great numbers but of inferior quality, not in
Athens only but in other centres of Hellenic

and Hellenistic culture. Even thereafter the production of new plays did not wholly cease, but continued sporadically until as late as the reign of Hadrian (117–138 A.D.). Moreover throughout this period from the fourth century onward the production of old plays, especially the tragedies of Euripides, was a prominent feature of dramatic festivals, and this custom of repeating ancient dramas survived, doubtless with decreasing frequency and ever diminishing popularity until even the fifth century of the Christian era.[12]

II. DRAMATIC ART AT ROME

OF THEMSELVES the Romans never developed a genuine dramatic literature. In the early days indeed potentially dramatic performances of an uncouth sort flourished among them, and for a time gave promise of attaining literary merit. But the brilliant splendor of plays imported from Greece prevented these from coming to full fruition.

It was not until after Tarentum, one of the most important centres of Hellenistic culture in the west, had succumbed to the irresistible power of Rome (272 B.C.), that the inhabitants of Latium began to be sensible of the influence of Greek literature and civilization. At first a tiny rivulet, this influence became during the terrific struggle of the first Punic War (264–241 B.C.) a stream of considerable size and force, and in time a mighty river. What more natural then than that the splendor of the *Ludi Romani* (p. 52), held in the year 240 B.C., the year following the stirring victory over the forces of Hanno, should be given an added brilliance by performances of Greek plays? On this occasion Livius Andronicus, a native of Tarentum, presented before Roman audiences a comedy and a tragedy, translated and adapted from the Greek, and thus inaugurated the first period of Roman literature. Henceforward tragedy and comedy in Rome were largely Greek in subject and form, though the language employed was Latin; and the performances of plays, modeled chiefly on Greek originals, became a regular feature of Roman games and festivals.[13]

But neither comedy nor tragedy of legitimate form succeeded in rooting themselves deeply in Roman soil; and during the first century of the Empire after a precarious existence of about three centuries both types of drama practically disappeared from the stage. Henceforth the magnificent theatres which the Romans had constructed and lavishly adorned with every form of artistic display at their command were dedicated chiefly to tragedians' solos, such as Nero was fond of rendering, farces and cheap burlesques, pantomimic performances and vulgar variety shows.

It was therefore during the prosperous years of the Republic before the Roman character began to be undermined by the insidious effects of a too rapid increase of wealth and expansion of power and the influx from abroad of unwonted luxuries and debasing vices, that the drama may be said to have flourished. In addition to the tragedies translated and adapted from Greek originals, a modified form dealing with episodes in local history and legend, and known as *fabulae praetextae* (so named from the *toga praetexta*, the Roman dress of dignity, worn by the actors) won their share of applause.[14] But even before the close of the Republic the demoralizing influence of the prevailing inordinate fondness for spectacle and gorgeous display began to work the destruction of tragic drama. Cicero in a letter to his friend Marius, in which he describes the dedication of the theatre of Pompey (55 B.C.), asks with disgust: " What pleasure is there in seeing six hundred mules in the *Clytemnestra* [of Accius] or three thousand bowls in the *Trojan Horse* [of Livius] or infantry and cavalry engaging in battle in gay-colored armor? " The spectacle, he says, was so magnificent as to destroy all cheerful enjoyment.[15] A generation or so later Horace wrote in a similar vein of bitter complaint. Even the knights, he says, find more enjoyment in the idle pleasures of sense than in true dramatic art. The delight of the ears has degenerated into mere pleasing of the eye.[16]

As in the case of tragedy, so in that of comedy there were two types. Those of Greek origin, called *fabulae palliatae* because the actors impersonated Greeks and so dressed in Greek garb, were borrowed from New Comedy (p. 9, and fig. 4). Of this type are all the extant plays of Plautus and of Terence. After the death of Terence (159 B.C.) a slightly different style of comedy based upon Roman and Italian life of the middle classes, and known as *fabulae togatae* became popular.[17] But their vogue was brief. During the closing years of the Republic they, like the *palliatae*, after which they had been modeled, and like the two types of tragedy, gradually became moribund.

Strange as it may seem, plays in Greek, or at any rate portions of plays in Greek, were presented in the theatres of Rome, a custom seemingly inaugurated by victorious generals within a century after the introduction by Livius of Greek drama in translation.[18] Julius Caesar and after him Augustus caused performances to be held in which " actors in all languages " (*omnium linguarum histriones*) took part.[19] That

FIGURE 3. ACTORS PREPARING FOR A SATYR-PLAY

From a vase found at Ruvo, now in Naples. Date about 400 B.C.

some of these were Greek there can be no question. Brutus on one occasion (44 B.C.) is said by Plutarch [20] to have brought from Naples, a Greek settlement, a company of the best actors he could find in that city; and there are many references in ancient literature and records in inscriptions which indicate that until at least the close of the second century after Christ Greek was frequently heard upon the Roman stage. Probably such performances were patronized chiefly by the Greek residents and by Romans of the educated classes. And yet we must remember that at this period there were in Rome many others also who were familiar with the Greek language. There is reason for believing, for instance, that the Jews in Rome spoke Greek almost exclusively.[21]

The native dramatic impulses had given rise to two forms of crude entertainment: the *versus Fescennini* and the *satura*. In addition to these, two imported forms enjoyed much popularity: the *mimus* or mime, and the *fabula Atellana;* the former introduced from the Greek colonies of Southern Italy and Sicily, the latter from the Oscans.

According to Horace [22] the Fescennine verses (so named either from Fescennium, a village in

Etruria, or from *fascinum*, a phallic symbol which was supposed to avert the evil eye) originated at the rural festivals of the harvest and vintage. Responsive in character and in the old Saturnian metre, they were at first wholly improvisational and abounded in coarse wit, personal banter, and rustic raillery, which in time possibly when they were transferred from the country districts to the city, degenerated into lampoons so virulent and scurrility so libellous, that a law was passed in their restraint.

An improved form of these *versus Fescennini*, combined with music and dancing in imitation of the performances rendered by Etruscan mummers or *ludiones*, gave rise to the *saturae* (sc. *fabulae*), medleys consisting of scenes from daily life, composed also in the Saturnian metre, but without a connected plot and characterized by much good-humored hilarity. The Etruscan dancers, whose entertainments gave the impulse to the development of the saturae, were brought to Rome for the first time in the year 364 B.C. on the occasion of a pestilence, in the futile hope that by this enrichment of the *Ludi Romani* (p. 52) the anger of the gods, who had supposedly caused the plague, might be placated; and a temporary stage, the first stage ever erected in Rome, was constructed for their use in the Circus Maximus. After the introduction of Greek literature, one hundred years later, the satura as a dramatic entertainment did not long survive and eventually disappeared from the stage.

Not so, however, the other types mentioned above, the Atellan play and the mime, which during the last century of the Republic gradually won their way to a prominent position in the affection of the populace. The Atellanae (so named from Atella, an Oscan town in Campania) were an improved kind of saturae. They were brought to Rome about two hundred years before Christ after the subjugation of Campania in the second Punic War, but were not given literary treatment until the time of Sulla (*c.* 100 B.C.). The plots, though simple, possessed more or less artistic unity and drew their subjects from the life of the country towns and villages. Unlike the other types of plays which have been mentioned, the Atellanae required the use of masks, since the actors represented conventional stock characters as in a Punch and Judy show. Of these characters four were especially prominent: Pappus the pantaloon, the stupid, swaggering fool Bucco, the blockhead

Maccus and Dossennus the hunchback and
cunning knave; personages analogous to the
characters in the Italian *Commedia dell' Arte*
and to the clown and harlequin of modern pantomimic show.[23]

The Atellanae were regularly of small com-
pass like our modern one-act plays and apparently were sometimes presented as *exodia* after
the conclusion of regular dramas. The evidence
for this however is not conclusive. Though they
continued to be performed until the latest
period of the Empire, they were early supplanted in popular favor by the mime, as we are
told by Cicero in a letter (46 B.C.) to his friend
L. Papirius Paetus.[24]

The mime was a crude farce presenting
scenes from low life and consisting of song,
dance and dialogue. Though of great antiquity
it was not cultivated by the Romans as a literary type until the last century of the Republic.
What it was like however in the early days may
be gathered from the *Symposium* of Xenophon
which charmingly describes a banquet supposedly given in the year 421 B.C. by the rich
Athenian Callias. For the amusement of his
guests Callias engaged a strolling show-man
from Syracuse who brought with him a boy, a

flute player and a dancing girl who was also a tumbler. After presenting a number of dances and acrobatic performances, such as turning somersaults into a circle of upright knives and out again, the troupe brought the performance to a close with a ballet representing the loves of Dionysus and Ariadne, whereupon the banqueters expressed their delight by loud applause and shouts of " encore."

Performances such as this were a favorite amusement among the Romans as among the Greeks, and seem to have formed the tap-root of the Roman mime. As the mime developed under the influence of other dramatic types it was admitted to the stage and once established maintained its popularity until the close of the Empire, not only in the west but throughout the east as well.

The mimes were a combination of ballet and harlequinade. During the life time of Cicero (106–43 B.C.) they appear to have been presented chiefly as interludes or as *exodia* (except at the festival of Flora [p. 54] when they were exhibited independently of other plays), and the actors were few in number. But under the Empire they enjoyed a much greater degree of independence, their scope was enlarged and the number of performers increased. The chief actor was known as an *archimimus;* the fat-cheeked booby with shaven head, as *stupidus* or *parasitus.* Masks were not worn and the actors regularly appeared with bare legs and feet, from which custom they were called *planipedes.* The performers, dressed in amusing costumes, carried on a dialogue in speech and song full of coarsest jokes and accompanied by grimaces and lascivious gestures and unrestrained horse-play, while a chorus of dancers, both male and female, followed the action with appropriate songs and movements to the music of the pipe. The gross buffooneries and obscene suggestiveness of these farces suited the degraded taste of the times and gave them a power over the multitudes which the more refined drama had not known even in the best days of the Republic. Their sensual appeal was enhanced by the presence of the female actors and dancers (*mimae*), women of low character and shameless audacity, who wantonly exhibited their beauty to the gaze of the applauding crowds.

Another type of entertainment in great favor during the period of the Empire was the pantomime (*pantomimus*). This was performed by an actor, or rather by a dancer, attended by a chorus of singers and an orchestra of string, brass and wind instruments, while a sort of clapper (*scabellum* or *scabillum*) worn under the foot was used to keep the rhythm of the music and the dance in perfect unison. The origin of this species of dramatic entertainment may be found in the manner of rendering the *cantica* or lyrical monologues of Roman comedy, which were sometimes presented by two persons, a singer and a dancer, performing together. According to Livy [25] this practice was instituted by Livius Andronicus (died about 204 B.C.) who was so frequently called upon to repeat such portions of his plays that finding his voice hoarse he hit upon the device of placing a boy in front of the musician to sing the solo while he himself acted the words of the song, with the result that his gestures were much more vigorous and expressive than they would otherwise have been. The pantomime was first cultivated as an independent art under Augustus about the year 22 B.C. by two Greek freedmen, Bathyllus of Alexandria and Pylades of Cilicia. Of these the former essayed comic pantomime, a type that never thrived and after the death of Bathyllus soon fell into disuse. Tragic pantomime, on the other hand, won instant approval and quickly attained a tremendous vogue.

The subjects were chosen sometimes from history or legend, but more frequently from mythology and were often of an amorous character. The libretto, *fabula saltica,* from a literary point of view was usually as worthless as the average moving-picture scenario, and consisted of the more sensational portions of a story strung together in a series of *cantica.* These were sung by the chorus, while the single dancer (*pantomimus*) represented the various characters, both male and female, as well as the plot, by the movements of the body. The illusion was usually enhanced, indeed, by change of costume and mask, but the success of the performance depended mainly on the skill of the pantomime in portraying character and suggesting situation. The language of movement and gesture became a fine art and elicited the praise of many an ancient author. Others, however, refer to the passion for pantomime as a disease and curse.[26] Though always more artistic than the mime and originally no doubt nobler in conception, pantomime too finally yielded to the degrading influences of the times and degenerated into exhibitions of seductive grace and lewd suggestiveness. Not only in Rome, but in time throughout the Empire, even in Greece itself, the immense popularity of these two types of ignoble and immoral shows swept regular drama from the public stage. " Ancient dramatic art ended its existence with a hideous, lascivious grimace." [27]

The drama finally flickered out in the sixth century. Then came the darkness of the barbaric night. Drama died, but acting of a certain sort continued. The *mimi*, despised, dispossessed, driven from the theatres, became wanderers on the face of the earth, itinerant merrymakers, tumblers, jesters, clowns, at country festivals and village fairs, in wayside taverns and great lords' castles. From the descendants of these lowly entertainers and those of the Teutonic *scôp* or bard there sprang the *ioculatores*, the *jongleurs*, the minstrels of the Middle Ages, through whom on the rebirth of the theatre the buffoons of antiquity influenced however slightly the reviving dramatic art.[28] But the connection of the *mimi* with modern drama is a fine-drawn filament, so tenuous at times as to be invisible; that of classical tragedy and comedy, a massive cable of steel. How this cable was laid we shall see in a later chapter.

III. DRAMATIC FESTIVALS:
ATHENS

GREEK drama in each of its forms was from the first associated with religion. A dramatic performance was a sacred ceremony. No matter how obscure in origin, all types came to maturity in connection with the cult of Dionysus, and it was probably this cult, as most believe, that gave Greek drama its birth.

As distinguished from the Olympian divinities of the Homeric pantheon, Dionysus was supposed to enter and take possession of his worshippers through a form of mystical communion, when these were in a state of ecstasy. Enthusiasm, that is the condition of having the god present within one, was a conspicuous characteristic of his worship. All forms of his worship contained an element of enthusiasm, inspiration; and it may have been this feature that led to impersonation and ultimately to the drama. At any rate Dionysus came to be regarded as the patron of dramatic poetry.

Among the various means employed to induce

such delirious excitement, to stimulate the appropriate religious emotion, the most efficacious was wine. And it was perhaps for this reason that Dionysus was conceived to be the god of wine, a function that was held to be his among the Thracians as later also among the Hellenes. In this capacity he most deeply impressed the religious imagination of his worshippers, so that in the literature after the days of Homer his name was closely associated with the grape. In many of the festivals held in his honor wine played an important part. But it cannot be too strongly emphasized that the association of Dionysus with wine is not sufficient to explain the rise of drama.

For Dionysus was not thought of merely as a god of wine and drinking. He appears to have been thought of also as a nature-deity, and his imagined potency as a god of the generative forces of life was symbolized by the phallus. Little wonder then that the rustic festivals in celebration of his greatness not only included songs and dances and simple peasant sports accompanied by drinking and innocent merriment, but were marked also by coarse jesting and obscenity attended by unrestrained license. The broad jokes, violent abusiveness and frank indecency of Old Comedy faithfully reproduced the spirit of these early phallic ceremonies.

Though the uncouth rural celebrations such as have been described furnished the impulse for the growth of drama, dramatic art was developed and perfected in connection with two annual festivals held in the city of Athens. The older of these, perhaps a rustic festival in origin, was known as the Lenaea, and was celebrated in honor of Dionysus Lenaeus. In the sixth century and possibly also during a portion of the fifth, this festival was observed in a sacred enclosure or precinct called the Lenaeum, the site of which is uncertain but is said to have been in or near the market-place (p. 71).[29] The Lenaea became in time primarily a dramatic festival, precisely how is not known. It was held in the winter season, about the end of January, a time of the year when there were few visitors in Athens, and it was in consequence of little interest to any except to the Athenians themselves.

Its importance as a dramatic festival began early in the sixth century, between 580 and 560 B.C., when voluntary performances of comuses (p. 7) were made a part of the program. After this there is a gap of more than a hundred years in our information. The earliest recorded date of the presentation of comedy at Athens, presumably under state supervision, is 487/6 B.C. But whether this was at the Lenaea or not is not certain. Sometime after the middle of the fifth century (442? B.C.) a contest of comic actors was established at this festival, and a little later (from about 433 B.C.) a contest of tragic actors. But in what year tragedy was added to the program is not know. The few records that have been preserved seem to indicate that only two poets competed for the tragic prize, each with a group of three plays. There is no evidence for the presentation of satyr-drama. In the case of comedy, five poets appear to have contended for the prize, each with a single play. But for about a generation, beginning in 428 or 427 B.C., that is during the exhausting years of the Peloponnesian War, the number of comic poets was reduced to three.[30] Dithyrambic choruses seem not to have been a part of the celebration, at any rate not until late times. Although the Lenaea continued to be observed until at least the second century after Christ, comparatively little is known about its history or the extent and arrangement of its program.

Far more important for the history of drama and more magnificent as a spectacle was the City Dionysia, known also as the Great Dionysia, or even simply as the Dionysia, celebrated in honor of Dionysus Eleuthereus. The epithet Eleuthereus probably means ' pertaining to Eleutherae,' a village on the northern border of Attica, whence sometime in the sixth (?) century B.C. this particular cult of Dionysus is said to have been introduced at Athens, and his *bretas,* or wooden statue, brought to the city and set up in a small temple erected for the purpose on the southeastern slope of the Acropolis (p. 71). A parcel of ground surrounding this new shrine was dedicated to the service of the god and was known henceforward as the precinct of Dionysus Eleuthereus. Adjoining this temple an orchestra was established, and it was here that the great theatre of Athens took shape (see figs. 9 and 10). Both temple and orchestra appear to have been built under the direction of the tyrant Pisistratus (540–528 B.C.).

At any rate it is well known that Pisistratus undertook to adorn the city with architectural monuments, and in other ways laid the foundations for the future literary and artistic supremacy of Athens. It may even be that the

City Dionysia was founded at his suggestion. If he did not establish this festival, as many believe, he was certainly instrumental in effecting its reorganization. In the year 535/4 B.C., while Pisistratus was still at the height of his power, the first contest in tragedy was held on the occasion of the City Dionysia and Thespis of Icaria (p. 8) was awarded the prize. From this time until even as late as the second century after Christ tragedy continued to be the leading feature of this celebration.

Little is known about the early history of the Dionysia. As Athens advanced in influence and wealth the program was enlarged and rendered more magnificent in keeping with the growing splendor and political importance of the state. Before the close of the sixth century (515? B.C.) satyr-drama was introduced. In 508 B.C. a contest of dithyrambic choruses of men was added and about 501 B.C. voluntary performances of comuses, from which comedy developed. The first recorded presentation of comedy (487/6 B.C.) mentioned above may have been at the City Dionysia. The festival was held in the spring, about the end of March, and lasted for five, possibly six, days. At this season the city was filled with visitors, and the

Athenians accordingly took advantage of the opportunity thus afforded to display the achievements of their city in literature and the other arts. During the continuance of the festivities business houses and courts of law were closed, and the entire populace gave itself up to the enjoyment of the feast of music and drama.

The festival began with a magnificent procession in honor of Dionysus Eleuthereus, a ceremony in which all classes of citizens, rich and poor alike, took part: priests and other officials dressed in gorgeous robes, young women bearing on their heads baskets containing implements for the sacrifices, young men with shields and spears, the members of the choral and dramatic groups gaily dressed in brilliant costumes, and thousands of others, men, women and children, in holiday attire. No doubt this procession vied in splendor with that other procession which took place once in four years in connection with the Panathenaea and which Phidias and his fellow sculptors gloriously immortalized on the inner frieze of the Parthenon.

The purpose of this part of the celebration was to escort the ancient image of Dionysus along the road toward Eleutherae and to conduct it again into the city in commemoration of the day when it was first brought to Athens and installed in its new shrine south of the Acropolis. Early in the morning the procession formed at the precinct of the god, the statue was removed from its pedestal and borne in triumph first to the market-place and then, after certain ceremonies, out of the city and as far as the Academy, where ancient olive trees afforded grateful shade. Here the statue was set up and sacrifices offered. Feasting and sports and good-humored revelry consumed the hours of the afternoon. As the day drew to its close the celebrants returned to the city bearing lighted torches and escorted the sacred image to the theatre where they placed it with suitable rites in or near the orchestra in preparation for the festivities which were to follow.

The second day from early morning until late in the afternoon was devoted in the main to dithyrambic contests, which possibly continued the third day also. There were five choruses of boys and five of men, each consisting of fifty choreutae, and each supplied by one of the ten tribes or political divisions of Attica. These were amateur performances and constituted a superb musical festival in which the entire community participated. As usual in the case of

[37]

choral lyrics the dithyramb was a combination of song and dance. A clarinet [2] furnished the musical accompaniment. The choruses adjudged the victors in the competitions received prizes.

Dramatic events occupied the last three days. These were preceded by a sacrifice and libation and certain proclamations of interest to the body politic. In the fifth century B.C. three poets competed for the tragic prize, each with three tragedies and a satyr-drama; for the prize in comedy five plays, presented by five separate poets, appear to have been exhibited, except that during the Peloponnesian War and possibly also for a few years after its conclusion (from 428? to 390? B.C.) the number was reduced to three.[30] The order of these events is not known with certainty. It is generally supposed, however, that on each of the three days there were five performances: first three tragedies and a satyr-drama by one of the tragic poets, presented in rapid succession, and in the afternoon, possibly after a brief interim, a comedy. When five comedies were included in the program two of these may have been presented on the day (or days?) devoted to the dithyrambic contests.

The group of four dramas exhibited by each of the tragic poets was known technically as a *didascalia* or teaching, because in early times at least the poet himself taught and trained his actors and choreutae. Late writers frequently employed also the term tetralogy to denote such a group when the constituent plays were connected in subject. A good example is afforded by the *Oedipodeia* of Aeschylus, presented in the year 467 B.C., which consisted of the *Laius, Oedipus, Seven against Thebes,* and the *Sphinx,* and dealt with the fortunes of Laius, king of Thebes. In like manner when the three tragedies only were related in subject they were spoken of as a trilogy. When these terms were first applied to groups of dramas is not known. Of the three best known tragic poets of Athens Aeschylus alone regularly composed connected trilogies and tetralogies; Sophocles seldom, if ever, did so; Euripides, apparently never.

The composition of the audience is somewhat in doubt, though the evidence is fairly clear that boys, women, and sometimes even slaves were included. The price of admission — except in the earliest days when entrance was free — came to be fixed at two obols (six cents, but equivalent in purchasing power to perhaps a dollar today) and the money thus received became the property of the lessee (*architecton, theatrônes*) of the theatre, who was under contract in consideration thereof to keep the building in repair. Many specimens of ancient theatre tickets are known, usually small leaden coins stamped with a theatrical emblem.

In the fifth century B.C. plays were rarely reproduced at either the City Dionysia or the Lenaea. The dramas of Aeschylus, however, enjoyed a special privilege. The amazing genius of this poet so dazzled the Athenians of his generation that shortly after his death (456 B.C.) a decree was passed permitting his dramas to be re-exhibited in competition with new plays. That this was done more than once during the succeeding fifty years is attested by several ancient writers. Aristophanes amusingly refers to the practice in two of his extant comedies.[31] We are told, furthermore, on the authority of Dicaearchus, a philosopher of the school of Aristotle, that the *Frogs* of Aristophanes so delighted the audience that it was actually performed a second time.[32] As the *Frogs* was originally acted at the Lenaea (405 B.C.), the repetition may have taken place at the City Dionysia two months later. But this was evidently exceptional. If,

FIGURE 4. A PERFORMANCE OF NEW COMEDY
From a photograph by Alinari of a relief in Naples

however, a drama was at first unsuccessful, it might be revised and offered again in competition, a concession of which playwrights often took advantage.

In the fourth century several significant changes were introduced. Thus in the year 386 B.C. an old tragedy was performed as an introduction to the regular competition, and henceforth this became the uniform practice. After the close of the fourth century, as the production of new tragedies diminished, the repetition of old plays acquired a steadily increasing importance (p. 16). This was probably true also of the Lenaean festival. A further modification affected satyr-drama. Instead of having each tragic poet exhibit a play of this type as an *exodium* to his group of tragedies, it became the custom to present a single satyric play at the beginning of the program preceding the old tragedy, an arrangement which continued in force apparently for several hundred years. In 339 B.C. another change was effected. The contest between the comic poets was preceded by the reproduction of a comedy which had been previously exhibited. The plays chosen for this purpose appear to have been uniformly selected from New Comedy (p. 9).

A few days before the beginning of the City Dionysia a ceremony of peculiar interest was held in the Odeum which adjoined the theatre (p. 77). This was known as the *Proagon* or "ceremony preceding the contest." On this occasion the tragic poets each accompanied by his choregus (p. 43), actors, and choreutae, all gorgeously appareled and with crowns upon their heads, presented themselves before the spectators, for the purpose evidently of acquainting the people with the names of the poets and of the others who were to engage in the contests, and with the titles of the plays which were to be performed. In the absence of newspapers and handbills a ceremony of this sort no doubt rendered a useful service. At the Proagon held in the spring of 406 B.C., shortly after the death of Euripides the aged Sophocles, then in his ninety-first year, appeared in robes of mourning, and his actors and choreutae without the usual crowns. The spectators, we are told, burst into tears.[33] It is probable, though not certain, that comic and dithyrambic poets and their companions also took part in the Proagon. Whether a similar ceremony preceded the Lenaea is not known.

In the festival itself each poet as his turn

came was summoned by a herald and after
about 425 B.C. it became customary also to
sound a blast on a trumpet. The order of the
contestants was determined by lot. The lot was
employed also in the selection of the judges,
and, apparently several times. A large group of
candidates was reduced by successive drawings
to a small number, presumably five. Those who
were adjudged victors — poets, choregi, and in
course of time also actors — were crowned with
garlands of ivy. But in the case of the poets the
ivy-wreath and the applause of the multitude
were not the victor's sole reward; each of the
contestants received a payment of money from
the state. And it is probable that when contests
in acting also were established (pp. 33, 132),
each of the protagonists, or leading actors, was
similarly rewarded.

As the City Dionysia and the Lenaea were
festivals in which the entire community participated, they were conducted under the supervision of state officials. The Archon Eponymus,
who was chairman of the Board of Archons and,
so to say, gave his name to the year in which he
held office, was in charge of the City Dionysia.
The Lenaea was under the care of the Archon
Basileus, or King-Archon, who had supervision

also of the mysteries at Eleusis and whose duties in general were religious in character or had to do with various offences against religion. It was the duty of the archon to select from those who applied for permission to compete, the requisite number of tragic and comic poets, a task no doubt of grave responsibility, and to assign to each by lot a choregus; and after the middle of the fifth century also, by the same method, a protagonist.

The choregus (χορηγός) was a citizen of wealth, who performed certain duties (see below) in preparation for a choral or dramatic performance, in the case of tragedy of a group of performances, and defrayed out of his own purse most of the expenses incurred. This service he was required by law to render to the state. The Athenians were in the habit of calling upon their rich citizens on many different occasions to perform special duties involving large financial outlay. The order of selection was fixed by law, and the service thus performed was known as a *leiturgia* (λειτουργία; English, "liturgy"). The particular form of leiturgia rendered by a choregus was called a *choregia*.

During the fifth century B.C., from sixteen to eighteen choregi were required annually for the

City Dionysia, one each for the tragic poets, the five (or three) comic poets, and the ten dithyrambic choruses; and for the Lenaean festival, after the introduction of tragedy, from five to seven.

The duties of the choregi must have been onerous and their expenses large. In the case of tragedy, as also of comedy, the choregus was required to select and pay the members of the chorus, purchase or rent their costumes, arrange for a room in which to hold rehearsals, hire a *didascalos* or trainer (except in the early times when the poet himself served in this capacity), secure the requisite number of persons to act as mutes, and provide their costumes. In addition he was probably required to supply any unusual properties which might be needed, hire the pipe-player, and, it may be, pay the salaries also of subordinate actors. The leading actors, or protagonists, appear to have been paid by the state, at least after the middle of the fifth century when actors' contests were established and the protagonists assigned to the poets by the archon. Before this time, however, when each poet selected his own protagonist, as Aeschylus is said to have done and Sophocles during the earlier years of his career, this ex-

pense also may have been borne by the choregus. Who it was that paid for the costumes of
the actors is not known.

Shortly before the close of the exhausting
Peloponnesian War (431–404 B.C.), when there
was a dearth of well-to-do citizens and the state
was struggling desperately to stave off ruin,
rather than omit the City Dionysia even for a
year the Athenians passed a law (406 B.C.) permitting two men to share the expenses of a
choregia. Each was known as a *synchoregus* and
their joint service as a *synchoregia*. Several instances of synchoregiae are recorded, but as
soon as circumstances warranted the old choregic system was restored.

Finally, during the last quarter of the fourth
century (c. 308 B.C.) the institution of the
choregia was abolished and an official, called an
Agonothetes (ἀγωνοθέτης), was chosen annually to perform the services previously rendered
by the several choregi. The person selected for
this responsible position was of course a man
of great wealth, but he was assisted in defray-
ing the expenses of his office by contributions
from the treasury of the state.

As the City Dionysia and the Lenaea were religious celebrations, any violation of their sanc-

tity, such as the seizure during the festival of a debtor's goods, or any personal insult committed against a participant whether poet, choregus, actor, choreutes, or even a mere spectator, was treated as an act of sacrilege and was punishable with severe penalties. That all matters of this sort and all instances of neglect of duty on the part of a magistrate or of unfairness of a judge might be reviewed and brought to account, a special assembly of the people was held in the theatre on the day following the festival. This was done at any rate in the case of the City Dionysia, and that the same practice obtained in connection with the Lenaea is altogether probable. Officials who had performed their duties particularly well were on this occasion publicly honored; on the other hand any instance of alleged mismanagement or unfairness was subjected to a searching inquiry. If the charges were sustained by a vote of the people, the case might be brought before a regular court for trial. Personal outrages committed during the festival were usually severely punished. Demosthenes in the speech against Midias, who had brutally assaulted him in the theatre while he was serving as choregus for a chorus of boys in the year 350 B.C., proposes death as a suitable punishment for Midias or at least confiscation of his entire estate. He reminds his hearers that a certain Ctesicles had been put to death for striking a personal enemy with a whip during the Dionysiac procession, and that the father of the Archon Eponymus of the year 363 B.C. had been condemned by the assembly for violently ejecting a spectator from the theatre for taking a seat to which he was not entitled.[34] In the latter case the matter never came to trial as the accused died before the suit could be brought up in court, so that we are left in doubt as to what punishment would have been inflicted had the man been adjudged guilty. All of these instances, however, serve to emphasize with vivid intensity the fact that in ancient Athens these choral and dramatic celebrations were not observed merely through a love of art or for popular amusement or pecuniary gain, but were sacred ceremonies, a form of divine worship.

In addition to these two annual Dionysiac festivals in Athens there were other festal gatherings in the various towns and country districts of Attica. These were known as Rural Dionysia and were held in the winter months. They were originally of purely local interest.

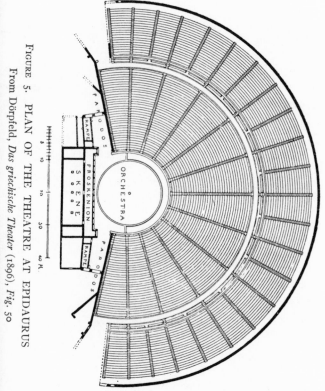

FIGURE 5. PLAN OF THE THEATRE AT EPIDAURUS

From Dörpfeld, *Das griechische Theater* (1896), *Fig.* 50

Gradually, however, under the influence of the Athenian Dionysia dramatic events became a central feature of many of these provincial celebrations, and their importance was correspondingly increased. The festival of this sort observed at the Piraeus, which was the port of Athens and virtually a part of the city, was especially famous and was supported by contributions from the state treasury. Many Athenians attended annually to take part in the procession and to witness the performances in the theatre. On the occasion of these various winter celebrations old plays which had been previously exhibited at Athens were performed again and again. Troupes of actors were organized and traveled from town to town, and this practice gave rise to the formation of a strong guild of actors known as the Artists of Dionysus (p. 132). By means of these revivals of plays at the Piraeus and elsewhere the Athenians and others became thoroughly familiar with the masterpieces of dramatic literature.

IV. DRAMATIC FESTIVALS: ROME

BEFORE the close of the fourth century B.C. dramatic festivals modeled on those at Athens had been established throughout most of the Greek world. These were at first regularly festivals of Dionysus. But this limitation soon proved too narrow, and the programs of many other religious and even secular celebrations, such as triumphs of generals, were enriched by the addition of dramatic performances.

This was the condition which obtained at Rome,[35] where the drama was quite dissociated from the worship of Dionysus. At Athens, as we have seen, there were but few days in the course of the year on which plays were presented, even if one include the festival at the Piraeus. In Rome, on the other hand, the relatively numerous public religious celebrations (*ludi publici*), together with the many games and contests supported by private munificence, including triumphs (*ludi votivi*), funerals of distinguished citizens (*ludi funebres*), and,

[50]

under the Empire, festivals arranged and given by magistrates and others for the purpose of courting popular favor (*ludi honorarii*), afforded many opportunities for witnessing theatrical exhibitions. Indeed, before the death of Sulla (78 B.C.) the *ludi publici* alone included forty-eight days on which entertainments were presented in the theatres, and the actor Roscius is believed to have appeared as many as one hundred twenty-five times in a single year.[36] After 50 B.C. many new festivals were instituted, the earliest being the *ludi Victoriae Caesaris* (or *ludi Veneris Genetricis*) celebrated by Julius Caesar on the occasion of the dedication of the temple of Venus Genetrix (46 B.C.), so that by the end of the Republic the annual games (*ludi sollemnes*) occupied altogether seventy-six days, of which fifty-five were devoted to dramatic performances (*ludi scaenici*). And in the fourth century after Christ, according to the calendar of Furius Dionysius Philocalus (354 A.D.), the number of regular holidays had increased to one hundred seventy-five or only a few days less than six months! Of these sixty-four were devoted to chariot-races, ten to gladiatorial shows, and one hundred one to theatrical entertainments. But there is little doubt that at this late date the last consisted chiefly of mimes and pantomimes.

The earliest of the public festivals at Rome which are of interest in connection with the drama was known as the *ludi Romani* and was observed in the month of September. Its origin is obscure, but the conjecture that the festival developed from *ludi votivi* has much in its favor. In any case, it was closely connected with the cult of Jupiter Capitolinus in whose honor a sacrificial banquet (*epulum Jovis*) was held on the Ides (13) of September, the dedication-day of the Capitoline temple. Originally of brief duration, perhaps only one day in length, the festival was gradually extended until in the Augustan era it included fifteen days (September 5–19). On the day following the *epulum* (i.e. September 14) was held a parade and review of horses (*equorum probatio*), presumably of the horses which were to be used during the succeeding days (15–19) in the chariot-races (*ludi circenses*). These races were held in the Circus Maximus in the long and narrow valley between the Aventine and the Palatine, and were preceded by a magnificent triumphal procession which set forth from the Capitol, passed along the Clivus Capitolinus, the Sacra Via and

FIGURE 6. THE THEATRE AT PRIENE

From Wiegand und Schrader, *Priene* (1904), *Fig.* 227

Vicus Tuscus to the Forum Boarium, whence it proceeded to the Circus, made a circuit of the arena, and halted before the magistrate's box near the entrance. The magistrate in charge headed the procession clad in the embroidered robes of a *triumphator*. There followed the youth of Rome, some on horseback, some on foot, charioteers with their chariots, horsemen, dancers, musicians, *collegia* of priests with the bearers of incense and sacred vessels, and lastly the images of the gods borne either on litters or in chariots driven by boys of noble birth both of whose parents were living.

The days preceding the Ides appear to have been devoted chiefly to dramatic performances (*ludi scaenici*), which dated back in the first instance to the exhibitions given by Etruscan *ludiones* in the year 364 B.C. (p. 22), but more particularly to the introduction of Greek drama in 240 B.C. by Livius Andronicus (p. 18). The *Phormio* of Terence was presented at the *ludi Romani* in the year 161 B.C., and in the following year the *Hecyra* (its second performance). The festival was presided over by the curule aediles.

Next in point of antiquity were the *ludi plebeii*, established in 220 B.C. and celebrated in

the month of November (4–17) in the Circus
Flaminius, which was situated in the southern
part of the Campus Martius just below the Capitoline hill. This festival was under the manage-
ment of the plebeian aediles and appears to have
been closely modeled after the *ludi Romani,* but
unfortunately little is known about it. There
was an *epulum Jovis* on the Ides (13) of the
month, and several of the days were dedicated
to dramatic entertainments. The *Stichus* of
Plautus was acted on the occasion of these *ludi*
in the year 200 B.C.

Other public celebrations at Rome important
in the history of the drama were the *ludi
Cereales* (April 12–19), a festival conducted in
honor of Ceres by the plebeian aediles; the *ludi
Florales* (April 28 to May 3), a sort of Bac-
chanalian carnival of the plebs during which
mimes were presented with gross indecency;
the *ludi Apollinares* (July 6–13), held in honor
of Apollo under the presidency of the *praetor
urbanus* and devoted chiefly to scenic performances, but including also chariot-races;
the *ludi Megalenses* (April 4–10), which were
pre-eminently scenic and were organized in the
year 204 B.C. in honor of Cybele, the Great
Mother of Mount Ida, whose worship was in-

troduced in this year from Phrygia and was the first of the oriental cults to establish itself at Rome; the *ludi Victoriae Sullanae* (October 26 to November 1), instituted by Sulla in memory of his victory at the Colline Gate (82 B.C.); and the *ludi Victoriae Caesaris* to which reference has already been made. These were originally held on the twenty-sixth of September, but were later transferred to July and extended to eleven days (July 20–30).

Mention should be made also of the *ludi Saeculares*, a festival celebrated theoretically once in one hundred years, but actually at irregular and usually briefer intervals.[37] To the student of Roman drama the most interesting observance of this jubilee was held in the year 17 B.C. under the presidency of the Emperor Augustus and his son-in-law and able general Agrippa. Extensive fragments discovered in 1890 of a marble column, which was erected in commemoration of the event and inscribed with a full account of the proceedings, corroborate and supplement the descriptions given by ancient writers.[38] The festival proper began on the evening of May 31 and continued without interruption for three nights and days (May 31 (evening) to June 3). Each evening and each morning sacrifices were offered to various divinities, and on the third day a hymn composed by the poet Horace (his *Carmen Saeculare*) was sung by twenty-seven boys and the same number of girls first on the Palatine at the temple of Apollo and again on the Capitoline hill in honor of Jupiter and his companion deities Juno and Minerva.

After the sacrifices of the first evening dramatic performances were held in the Campus Martius on a temporary stage with no seats provided for the spectators, as had been the custom in the time of Plautus, and these were continued during the following days and nights, but were transferred after the first night to a wooden theatre also in the Campus Martius near the Tiber. These performances are designated in the inscription *Ludi Latini,* by which is meant no doubt *fabulae praetextae* and *togatae,* perhaps also Atellan plays and mimes (p. 21). The celebration was brought to an end with games in a temporary circus near the theatre.

On the second day after the close of the festival and continuing for seven days (June 5–11) were held *ludi honorarii,* consisting of musical and dramatic entertainments of three types: *ludi Latini* in the wooden theatre just mentioned; *ludi Graeci thymelici,* performances of song and dance, in the theatre of Pompey (p. 19); and lastly *ludi Graeci astici* " in the theatre which is in the Circus Flaminius," [39] probably the unfinished theatre of Marcellus (p. 98). The expression *Graeci astici* is plainly reminiscent of the Athenian City Dionysia and may be interpreted to mean Greek dramas translated and adapted by Roman playwrights.[40]

The expenses entailed by these many public festivals as well as by the innumerable private celebrations were enormous, but what proportion of the expenditures was required for the dramatic exhibitions can unfortunately no longer be determined. The presentation of plays at night time by the light of blazing torches in the *ludi Saeculares* — exceptional though it was — seems very modern and may serve to remind us that in general dramatic entertainments at Rome were conducted in a manner far more like that which obtains today than were the tragic and comic contests at Athens.

In the latter city, as we recall, the poets made application to the archon in charge for permission to present his plays. The festivals were held in honor of Dionysus, and Dionysus alone;

private citizens of wealth were compelled by law to bear the greater part of the financial burdens; poets, choregi and actors competed for prizes, which were awarded by a panel, or panels, of judges; and the entire celebration was supervised by a state official as an act of public worship. All of the participants were for the time being sacrosanct.

In Rome, on the other hand, although plays were regularly a part of religious festivals, their connection with religion was far less intimate. The magistrates in charge of games arranged with a professional manager (*dominus*) of a theatrical company (*grex*) for the exhibitions desired. The manager, known also as *actor*, was generally a freedman. The actors were regularly freedmen, foreigners, or slaves, who were either the property of the manager or were hired for the occasion. The manager bought plays outright from the poets and assumed entire charge of the performances, including the arrangements for costumes and properties which were provided by a purveyor (*conductor* or *choregus*). He also assumed the financial risk of the venture, and was compensated by the givers of the games (*ludorum datores*) according to the success of the performance. The managers, moreover, were often themselves actors. Naturally then there was keen rivalry between them as also between other leading actors for popular favor, and *claques* were organized to support certain actors and to shout down their opponents, a practice that sometimes resulted in riots and the consequent punishment, even banishment, of actors and their adherents.[41] Those who were adjudged most successful sometimes received prizes of palm leaves and crowns of gold or silver, and under the Empire even money and articles of clothing. But there never were at Rome such systematic competitions under state supervision as existed at Athens.

Dramatic entertainments were regularly held in the daytime and were announced by public criers (*praecones*). As a play was about to begin announcement was made of its title, the author's name, and similar matters of interest to the public. Frequently too there was an appeal for a silent and respectful hearing, a wise precaution as Roman audiences included many who were inclined to boisterous and turbulent conduct. Indeed, so restive and fickle were the spectators that even when a comedy was in progress they sometimes bolted from the theatre in a body for a more exciting diversion. When

Terence first presented the *Hecyra* (165 B.C.) the audience got wind of a boxing bout and an exhibition of rope-dancing. In a twinkling the theatre was empty. A second attempt five years later fared no better; rumor of a gladiatorial show set the house in an uproar.[42] Little wonder then that actors and managers were nervous, little wonder that they pleaded for silence and good behavior. But so did performers of ecclesiastical plays in the Middle Ages. So did even Shakespeare. And with reason. The groundlings who, as Hamlet complained,[43] were " for the most part capable of nothing but inexplicable dumb shows and noise," might at any moment hiss and hoot or raise even a more serious disturbance. The rabble before whom Plautus and Terence presented their plays did not greatly differ from the motley crowds that filled the pit of the " Swan " or " Fortune," or from the bear-baiting " fans " of the Bankside.

V. THE GREEK THEATRE: ITS ESSENTIAL FEATURES; DEVELOPMENT AND SUCCESSIVE TRANSFORMATIONS

THE history of the theatre, as of dramatic literature, begins in ancient Greece and in particular in Athens. One is very apt nowadays looking back through the long vista of twenty centuries to regard the Greek theatre as a fixed type. In fact, however, no two ancient Greek theatres were exactly alike, and when the history of each is considered one discovers that the various forms, which when reduced to simplest terms constitute for us the normal type, were the result of gradual changes and repeated readjustments. The early formative period during which this normal type was evolved extended through many decades.

The essential features of the structure which resulted from this process of development were three in number (fig. 5): orchestra (ὀρχήστρα, "dancing-place") with two approaches, one from either side, known as *eisodi* or more commonly as *parodi* (εἴσοδος "entrance"; πάροδος, "side entrance"); *theatron* or auditorium (θέατρον, "viewing place"); and *skene* or scene-building (σκηνή, "shelter," or "hut"). These component elements, though essential to the perfected structure, were conjoined by a process of accretion and never cohered to form a single architectural unit.

In point of chronology the orchestra was the earliest portion, the nuclear centre of the aggregate. About its circle in the early days the spectators stood or sat during the performance of the choral dances from which in the course of time, both tragedy and comedy evolved, and apparently for many decades, possibly even centuries, after the erection of auditorium and scene-building the orchestra-area still continued to be the focus of the theatre not merely in a physical sense but from the point of view of the action as well (p. 101). Its surface was merely hardened earth, and that portion of its circle which was included within the area of the auditorium was marked out by a low curb, surrounded in turn in some theatres by a deep gutter and a broad passageway between gutter and seats, as at Athens (fig. 9), in others only

[62]

by a passageway which served also as a drain, as at Epidaurus (figs. 1 and 5). In the latter theatre the curb was continued to form a complete circle, but this appears to have been exceptional. The sole permanent accessory of the orchestra was an altar or *thymele* ($\theta \upsilon \mu \acute{\epsilon} \lambda \eta$), which stood either at its centre or at some point on its periphery (fig. 6; see also p. 101).

The first addition to the orchestra was the auditorium, which consisted in early times in part of wooden seats, in part of the rising ground of a convenient hillside. Later these simple accommodations gave way to elaborate structures of masonry. In some instances seats were carved out of the native rock, as in the uppermost portion of the fourth-century auditorium at Athens, also at Argos, Chaeronea, and most notably of all in the theatre at Syracuse (Sicily) where almost the entire building was constructed in this fashion.

The auditorium was the most conspicuous and still remains in the majority of instances the most prominent and impressive feature of the theatres whose ruins dot the landscape of the Hellenic world (fig. 1). Although usually somewhat larger than a semicircle and otherwise

[63]

symmetrical, it was sometimes quite irregular in shape, as at Delos and Athens and in the tiny theatre in the village of Thoricus on the southeastern coast of Attica (fig. 7).

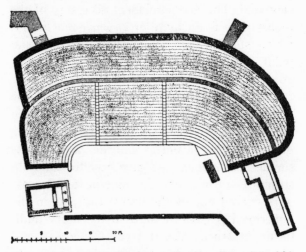

Fig. 7. Plan of the Theatre at Thoricus. From Dörpfeld, *Das griechische Theater* (1896), *Fig.* 43

Whatever its shape or size the auditorium, like the orchestra, was never provided with a roof (for the use of an awning in Roman times see p. 91). The seats were divided into wedge-shaped sections by means of radiating aisles, and were usually further divided by one or more curving, horizontal passageways known as *dia-zômata* (διάζωμα, " a girdle "). The front row of seats regularly constituted a *proëdria* or place of special honor and as such consisted of thrones (Athens, fig. 9), or of ornate benches (Megalopolis, Sicyon). At Epidaurus similar benches stood also immediately below and above the diazoma (figs. 1 and 5). At Oropus and Priene the proëdria was at the edge of the orchestra-circle (fig. 6). In late times new seats for dignitaries were not infrequently constructed on a level with the top of the *proskenion* (see below), or of the stage.

Access to the auditorium was chiefly through the parodi and orchestra. Large theatres how-ever, and sometimes smaller ones as well, had also stairways or ramps leading to the upper banks of seats. At Sicyon tunnels were cut for this purpose through the hill, one from either side, but whether these were a part of the orig-inal structure or were added in the Roman pe-riod has not yet been determined.

Opposite the auditorium stood the *skene* or scene-building which served in the first instance as a background for the actors and provided accommodations for dressing-rooms and per-haps also for the storing of various properties.

It was of a rectangular shape, sometimes with projecting wings known as *paraskenia* (singular, *paraskenion*, παρασκήνιον) at the sides (fig. 12), and in the Hellenic and Hellenistic periods it was connected with the auditorium, if at all, only by a gateway at either end (figs. 1 and 5), and it was seldom, if ever, more than two stories in height. Originally constructed of wood or of other perishable materials the scene-building was at first temporary in character; apparently not until the fourth century was a skene of stone erected. Its shape and its appearance in the fifth century are not known. In Hellenistic times and possibly also in the earlier period, there stood in front of the lower story of the scene-building a row of columns or rectangular pillars with attached semi-columns (figs. 6 and 8), surmounted by an entablature and provided with doors and movable panels of wood in the intercolumniations. The flat, or nearly flat, roof supported by this colonnade constituted a long and narrow platform. This portion of the building was known as the *proskenion* (fig. 5), or in the later centuries at least also as *logeion* (i.e. " speaking place "; λογεῖον from λέγω, " I speak "); and the question as to its origin and purpose is one of the most difficult as well as

[66]

one of the most important problems in the history of the scene-building (p. 90).[44] The best preserved example is found in the small theatre at Priene in Asia Minor (fig. 6), but the others can be restored with more or less accuracy from existing fragments (fig. 8). In some theatres ramps led up to the top of the proskenion from either side, as at Epidaurus (fig. 5) and Sicyon; [45] in others there were steps at the side or rear; in still others, a stairway or stairways in the interior of the scene-building. In the Hellenistic period too, perhaps earlier as well, the façade of the upper story or *episkenion* (ἐπι-σκήνιον) appears to have been pierced by one or more large openings fitted with folding doors or *thyromata* (θυρώματα); see fig. 8, and page 90.[46]

But throughout the Hellenistic age the theatre continued to be bi-partite, and the skene relatively small and simple both in arrangement and appearance. Not until the Roman era were these various component elements, scene-building and auditorium with the orchestra between, welded into a single structure possessing genuine architectural unity such as appears in the imposing theatres at Orange in southern France (fig. 18) and at Aspendus on the southern coast of Asia Minor (fig. 17). In the same period, too, the scene-building, which by then certainly had

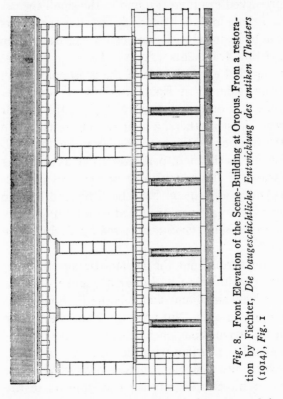

Fig. 8. Front Elevation of the Scene-Building at Oropus. From a restoration by Fiechter, *Die baugeschichtliche Entwicklung des antiken Theaters* (1914), *Fig.* 1

become a stage-building, was enlarged and its façade sumptuously adorned (fig. 17).

FIGURE 9.   THE THEATRE AT ATHENS, ORCHESTRA–AREA AND
REMAINS OF THE SCENE–BUILDING

From a photograph by Mrs. John Lyttle, April, 1925

The development and successive transformations of the Greek theatre thus briefly outlined
are well illustrated by the Dionysiac theatre at
Athens, which is the only Greek theatre whose
growth can at present be traced even meagrely
during the formative period. For this reason and
also because it seems to have served as the
model after which, though with infinite variety
of detail, subsequent Greek and to a large extent even Roman theatres were patterned and
because it was here that Aeschylus, Sophocles,
Euripides, and Aristophanes, not to mention the
host of other tragic and comic poets of ancient
Athens, presented most, if indeed not all, of
their plays, this building occupies a unique position in the history of the stage. Moreover, it
continued in use for dramatic and other performances and spectacles and for other public
functions for at least one thousand years, so
that not only does its appeal to the imagination
far surpass that of any other structure of the
kind, but it has been in point of influence the
most important theatre in the world. These
facts justify a rather full account of its history
and a somewhat detailed description of its ruins,
to which we may now turn.

VI. THE THEATRE OF DIONYSUS AT ATHENS

UNDER the able administration of Pisistratus during the third quarter of the sixth century before Christ Athens emerged from the provincialism and comparative obscurity which had been her lot and entered upon a career of leadership in literature and the other arts that made her in the words of the Thucydidean Pericles "the school of Hellas." [47] She became

> *Athens, the eye of Greece, mother of arts*
> *And eloquence.*[48]

One of the many activities of this benevolent "tyrant" concerned itself, as we have seen (p. 34), with the important choral and dramatic festival known as the City Dionysia, in connection with which apparently the small temple of Dionysus Eleuthereus in the precinct on the southeastern slope of the Acropolis was erected to receive the image of the god brought from Eleutherae, and the theatre in the same precinct established (figs. 9 and 10). At any rate, temple and theatre belong together and both date from the sixth century, as the extant portion of the former and the oldest remains of the latter make abundantly clear.

Earlier in the century dramatic and choral performances had been held in an orchestra adjoining the market-place *north* of the Acropolis, where a rude auditorium of wooden seats was erected on a hill-slope. The exact site of this old orchestra and *theatron* has not yet been determined, but apparently it was early deemed inadequate or for some other reason considered unsuitable. Decision was made therefore to move the theatre to a more favorable location, and the site selected for the new structure was the precinct of Dionysus on the southeastern slope of the Acropolis. In striking contrast with the Elizabethan theatres at London, which were erected outside the city limits beyond the jurisdiction of the city corporation, the theatre at Athens was not only in the city, but even in one of the most important of its many sacred demesnes. Moreover the priest of Dionysus Eleuthereus was assigned in the new auditorium the place of greatest honor, the central seat of the

first row (see p. 82). The intimate connection between religion and the drama in ancient
Greece could hardly be more clearly indicated.

The ruins of the Athenian theatre are ex-
tremely complicated (fig. 9). The skene in particular, repeatedly remodeled, survives as a bewildering tangle of walls differing in material
and mode of construction, the interpretation of
which is fraught with difficulties. Even auditorium and orchestra present serious problems.
And yet, though the exact appearance of the
entire structure at any one time can no longer
be recovered, several periods in its history are
clearly distinguishable.

The earliest of all, extending from the days of
Pisistratus and Thespis to the midpoint of Aeschylus' career, roughly the last third of the
sixth century B.C. and the first two or three
decades of the fifth, is represented by very
scanty remains: a simple auditorium resting on
the hillside, probably shallower and more elon-
gated than that of later times, and provided
with wooden seats; a large circular orchestra
the southern portion of which formed a terrace
some six or seven feet above the sloping terrain
(fig. 10); and two parodi, or, as some believe,
only one parodos, supported like the orchestra-

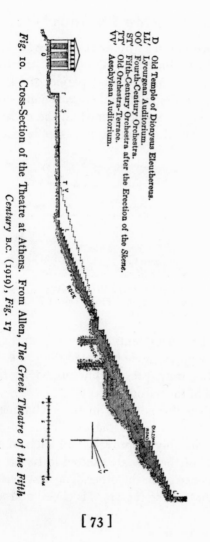

D Old Temple of Dionysus Eleuthereus.
LL' Lycurgean Auditorium.
OO Fourth-Century Orchestra.
ST Fifth-Century Orchestra.
TT' Old Orchestra-Terrace after the Erection of the *Skene*.
VV' Aeschylean Auditorium.

Fig. 10. Cross-Section of the Theatre at Athens. From Allen, *The Greek Theatre of the Fifth Century* B.C. (1919), *Fig.* 17

terrace (fig. 11) by a retaining wall of reddish Acropolis limestone — such was the theatre at Athens during the first period of its development. Scene-building there was none, nor stage; the plays were performed on the orchestra-terrace. An altar and a few simple accessories,

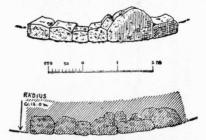

Fig. 11. Portion of the Retaining Wall of the Old Orchestra-Terrace at Athens. From Dörpfeld, *Das griechische Theater* (1896), *Fig.* 6

interpreted by hints and descriptions contained in the plays, alone indicated the scene. Dressing booths were presumably placed at the outer ends of the parodi.

With the advance in the technique of dramatic composition the conditions of presentation steadily improved, and each of these aspects of the new art exerted in turn a powerful influence upon the other. The first period in the history of the theatre was closed and a new era

opened with the erection of a scene-building.
Precisely when this took place cannot now be
determined, though it was certainly earlier than
458 B.C. in which year Aeschylus presented his
famous and still extant Orestean trilogy consisting of the *Agamemnon, Choephori,* and *Eumenides,* the first two of which required a palace,
the last a temple. Moreover the opening scene
of the *Agamemnon* was upon the roof of the
palace, while the action of the *Choephori* made
necessary the use of several doors. Evidently
the scene-building was already a substantial
structure of considerable size, and was erected
in all likelihood upon the orchestra-terrace in
the segment of the circle south of the line of the
parodi. Constructed of perishable materials it
has of course entirely disappeared. There are no
archaeological remains which can with certainty
be assigned to this period. Yet clearly the addition of so important a feature as a scene-
building, however unpretentious it may have
been at first, was an event of epochal significance.

Another epoch-making innovation of this
time, if ancient testimony may be trusted, was
the use of painted scenery. According to Aristotle [49] Sophocles led the way, while Vitruvius

states that the artist Agatharchus painted a scene (*scaenam fecit*) when Aeschylus was bringing out a tragedy and left a commentary about it.[50] " This led Democritus and Anaxagoras," he continues, " to write on the same subject, showing how, given a centre in a definite place, the lines should naturally correspond with due regard to the points of sight and the divergence of visual rays, so that by this deception a faithful representation of the appearance of buildings might be given in painted scenery, and so that, though all is drawn on a vertical flat façade, some parts may seem to be withdrawing into the background and others to be standing out in front." These words suggest that Agatharchus was a discoverer of the principles of linear perspective. But this almost passes belief. Precisely what the nature of his scene-painting was, what the advance in technique that he achieved, no one knows. Perhaps the latter was merely a form of linear symmetry and a more telling use of complementary colors. Yet one enthusiastic but competent critic writes: " The fame of Agatharchus will live, not by the work of his after years, however much sought for his decorations may have been, but by what he created in the freshness of his youth, a scene that lasted one single day, but revolutionized art for ever and probably even altered in time our vision itself." [51]

Be this as it may, the brief span of years covered by the second quarter of the fifth century constitutes a memorable period in the annals of the theatre. Then came an era of expansion and reconstruction, affecting not the theatre only but the entire precinct (fig. 10). The position of the theatre was shifted, slightly to the west, somewhat more to the north, and an auditorium of stone begun; to the south of the new orchestra a long colonnade of gleaming marble was built; to the south of this in turn and parallel thereto a larger and more splendid temple to house a chryselephantine statue of the god by the sculptor Alcamenes. [52]

At the same time, or perhaps a decade or two earlier than these changes, in the area east of the precinct and adjoining the theatre there was erected an Odeum or Music Hall, one of the many notable public edifices with which Pericles, statesman and patron of the arts, adorned his native city. [53] Recent excavations, still unfinished, have brought to light a portion of this famous building. It was a large, rectangular structure with a high peaked roof made from

[77]

the masts and yards of Persian ships, relics of the battle of Salamis (480 B.C.). Within were many columns and tiers of seats arranged on a sloping floor constituting a sort of indoor theatre where were held contests in musical skill and other concerts and meetings of various kinds, among them the annual gathering known as the Proagon (p. 42). Similar hypostyle halls were not uncommon in ancient Greece, such as the sanctuary of the mysteries at Eleusis, and the Hall of the Ten Thousand adjoining the theatre at Megalopolis.

The Odeum of Pericles was planned and built about the middle of the century, certainly not later than the spring of 441 B.C. Whether the reconstruction of the theatre was begun at this time and the colonnade and temple, mentioned above, erected is uncertain. But whatever its date the new auditorium appears never to have been completed, and later was again remodeled.

All traces of the scene-building have vanished. Its size, shape, and appearance must therefore remain in doubt. Probably it was of wood, and one may conjecture that it resembled the skene of the Hellenistic age, but with deep paraskenia as in the scene-building of the fourth century (fig. 12). One point however is clear: there is no archaeological evidence and no trustworthy literary evidence for the existence of a stage at this period.[54] The orchestra-area presumably continued as before to be the chief place of action, where actors and chorus

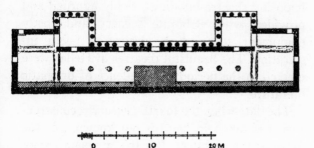

Fig. 12. Plan of the Fourth-Century *Skene* of the Theatre at Athens. From a conjectural restoration by Dörpfeld, *Das griechische Theater* (1896), *Taf.* II

mingled freely together. The scene-building, though constantly used, was still in large degree merely an adjunct.

Throughout the fifth century, the most fecund and brilliant century in the annals of ancient drama, progress in the physical conditions of presentation did not keep pace with the development of dramatic art. At the close of the century the theatre at Athens was still unfin-

[79]

ished and was in part of wood. An hundred years later when tragedy was moribund and Philemon, Menander and others were amusing the Athenians with second-rate comedies, it was a superb edifice of stone and marble. In ancient Greece as later in northern Europe the age of imposing theatre-buildings, richly adorned and provided with elaborate scenery and costly equipment, followed the decline of poetic inspiration. The beautiful theatres of Hellas were erected in the period of decadence of dramatic literature.

The date when the fourth-century reconstruction was taken in hand is not known, nor the name of the architect. But that it was a reconstruction and not merely the completing of a task already commenced has been shown beyond a peradventure by recent excavations. The position of the theatre appears to have been again shifted, this time about two metres to the north; along its southern line the unfinished auditorium of the fifth century was cut back and new retaining walls set up; the great outer wall on the western side constructed and perhaps at the same time the eastern half of the auditorium extended and given the irregular shape which it still retains; the beautiful marble thrones, which constitute the front row of seats, erected and a skene built of stone and marble. Not until the administration of Lycurgus, minister of finance from 338 to 326 B.C., was the work brought to an end. For this reason the building is frequently referred to nowadays as the theatre of Lycurgus or the Lycurgean theatre. Its completion was synchronous with the rise of New Comedy (p. 9).

The vast auditorium with its massive retaining walls of limestone and conglomerate rock and its seventy-eight(?) tiers of seats arranged in thirteen wedge-shaped sections extended even to the scarp of the Acropolis and was quite irregular in shape, especially on the eastern side where it adjoined and partially enclosed the Music Hall of Pericles. The seating capacity did not exceed seventeen thousand. For a considerable distance along the northern edge the rock at the base of the cliff was cut away to make room for the uppermost banks of seats. This spot was therefore known as the *katatome* or the Cutting. Near its centre was a grotto which a certain Thrasyllus enlarged and adorned with an elaborate choregic monument to commemorate his victory with a chorus of men in the year

319 B.C. Today this grotto is a much-frequented shrine of the Virgin. In the region of the kata-tome the seats were hewn out of the native rock; elsewhere they were constructed of lime-stone blocks, placed either directly on the earth or, in some portions, on foundations of conglom-erate. As they are only about fifteen inches in height we may assume that the spectators were in the habit of bringing rugs and cushions with them. The marble thrones, sixty-seven in num-ber, were reserved for the use of the more prominent priests and other officials of the city. The throne in the exact centre, slightly larger than the others and most ornate of all and provided with a canopy, was appropri-ately assigned to the priest of Dionysus Eleuthereus as the inscription on the front still attests.

The skene unfortunately has perished except for portions of the foundations and a few pieces of the superstructure. But it was evidently a large rectangular building with remarkably deep paraskenia (fig. 12), which some would restore as towers. According to another inter-pretation however they were not above one story in height and were adorned, each of them, with six small Doric columns and simple Doric frieze (fig. 13). The restoration of the central portion also is in doubt. No remains have been found of a proskenion belonging to this period, and nothing of the upper story or episkenion. Quite unwarranted however is the assumption of a stage. Probably the whole resembled the

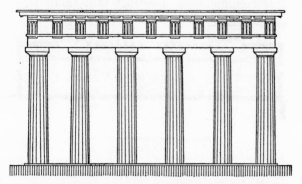

Fig. 13. Doric Columns of a *Paraskenion* of the Lycurgean Theatre at Athens. After Fiechter, *Die baugeschichtliche Entwicklung des antiken Theaters* (1914), *Fig.* 12

scene-building of the fifth century on the one hand, on the other that of the Hellenistic age. But proof is lacking.

The Lycurgean skene continued in use apparently for about two hundred years (some would say two hundred fifty years), then came the Hellenistic remodelment. The paraskenia were made shallower (fig. 14) and were adorned, as presumably they had previously been adorned, with Doric columns of Pentelic marble, portions of two of which are still standing (fig. 9). Between the paraskenia was erected a marble proskenion with a door in the central intercolumniation. The fact that there was a

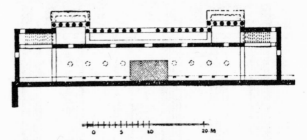

Fig. 14. Plan of the Hellenistic Scene-Building at Athens. From a restoration by Dörpfeld, *Das griechische Theater* (1896), *Fig.* 26

door suggests that the other intercolumnar spaces were closed with panels, as in other Hellenistic proskenia. But at Athens these spaces were remarkably narrow in proportion to their height and to the width of the intervening columns.[55] The upper story was no doubt of stone or marble with a façade consisting of alternate piers and thyromata as in the theatres at Oropus, Priene, Ephesus, etc. (fig. 8). Whether at

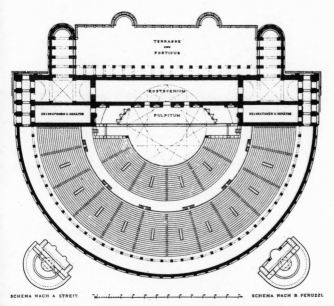

FIGURE 15. PLAN OF THE THEATRE OF
MARCELLUS AT ROME

From Streit, *Das Theater* (1903), *Taf.* VIII

this time the top of the proskenion served commonly as a stage is a question still in dispute (p. 90).

After another long interval the theatre was again reconstructed, this time under Roman influence in honor of the Emperor Nero who visited Athens in 67 A.D. With this remodelment it became a quasi-Roman theatre (p. 93), with presumably a deep and low stage, not above five feet in height, extending a considerable distance into the orchestra-area [56] while at the rear of the stage arose a lofty proscenium-façade consisting of projecting and receding members lavishly ornamented with columns and statues, and supported by a new massive foundation of large rectangular limestone blocks, many of which are still *in situ*. Numerous fragments of the superstructure, some of Pentelic, some of Hymettic marble — huge elliptical columns, pillars with attached semi-columns of the Corinthian order, arches carved in some instances from a single piece, enormous architrave blocks (see fig. 9.) — bear eloquent testimony to the splendor, the truly regal magnificence, of this Neronian building. The orchestra was paved with marble slabs, those at the centre, white, bluish and pink, arranged in the form of a rhom-

boid with a round depression at the middle point
to receive the base of a small altar. The open
portions of the gutter were covered with a pave-
ment of marble blocks; and just beyond, no
doubt to protect the audience from injury in the
case of gladiatorial combats and similar spectacles, was erected a beautiful balustrade also
of marble most of which fortunately is still
intact (fig. 9).

The Neronian skene must have been very imposing, far more so than its predecessors had
been, and continued in use with apparently only
slight changes for several hundreds of years.
Indeed none of the alterations made in the
theatre after the time of Nero were of fundamental consequence. During the reign of Hadrian (117–138 A.D.) some of the thrones were
removed to make room for a splendid royal box
(*tribunal*), and thirteen statues of the Emperor
were set up, one in the centre of each wedge of
seats.[57] Later, in the third or fourth century
A.D., a certain Phaedrus, governor of Attica, rebuilt the stage and made the orchestra water-
tight that it might on occasion be flooded for
mimic sea battles! The stage (fig. 9), four feet,
three inches in height, extended beyond the
inner line of the parodi and joined the ex-

tremities of the Neronian balustrade, as indeed Nero's stage also may have done. The front was adorned on either side of the central steps with statues placed in niches (a kneeling Silenus still occupies one of them) and a frieze of eight large slabs of marble sculptured in high relief. The four which survive bear figures portraying the birth of Dionysus, the introduction of his cult into Attica, and other events not easy to interpret connected with his worship at Athens especially as patron of the drama (fig. 9).

This frieze appears to date from the time of Nero; very likely it adorned the Neronian stage. In the Phaedrian reconstruction the blocks at the back of the figures were cut down and new cornice blocks superimposed, whose overhanging portions almost rested on the heads of the statues. Long afterward when finally the theatre had fallen into decay the heads of all the figures, including even that of the goat on the second slab, were knocked off — an act of wanton vandalism. Today the weird and melancholy appearance which the frieze presents may symbolize for us the decadence of dramatic art during the Roman Empire.[58]

VII. GRAECO-ROMAN AND ROMAN
THEATRES

DURING the course of the fifth century B.C. other theatres than that at Athens were constructed in various parts of the Greek world, but unfortunately little is known about them. The tiny theatre at Thoricus in Attica (fig. 7) may have been one of these, as also that at Eretria on the island of Euboea. Thucydides[59] mentions a Dionysiac theatre at the Piraeus. Apparently one of the earliest of all was at Syracuse, Sicily, where Aeschylus at the request of Hiero presented his *Women of Aetna* in 476 B.C. and a few years later his *Persians*. The development of this building, however, cannot be traced until a very much later period.

In the fourth and following centuries theatres were erected in great number, no two of which were alike in all details though similar in essential features. Of these one of the most beautiful was that at Epidaurus in the Peloponnesus, built about 350(?) B.C. under the direction of the architect Polyclitus the younger (figs. 1 and 5). The scene-building designed and constructed by Polyclitus can no longer be restored, though it may have resembled that at Athens. The Ionic proskenion apparently dates from the Hellenistic era. At either end of the skene stood a double gateway, one door of which opened upon the parodos, the other upon a ramp which led to the top of the proskenion. For some reason this theatre was never reconstructed under Roman influence, but remained throughout the period of the Empire a building of the Hellenistic type.

Beginning about the time of the establishment of the Empire, however, possibly earlier in some instances, many Greek theatres were remodeled as was that at Athens, and made to conform more or less closely to the Roman style of structure. As the process of modernization was carried farther in some cases than in others and as no two of the reconstructed buildings were exactly alike, it is difficult to group them all under a single designation. But what took place can be easily explained if we first summarize the differentiating characteristics of the Hellenistic and Roman types.

The Hellenistic theatre, like the Hellenic, was

in reality a combination of two structures,
scene-building and auditorium, placed in jux-
taposition with uncovered passageways or
parodi between. The auditorium was usually
built upon a hillside and, like the orchestra-
area which it enclosed, was uniformly larger
than a semi-circle. The skene was comparatively small and not more than two stories in
height. In the theatres of Greece and Asia
Minor the façade of the lower story of the
scene-building was a proskenion-colonnade with
panels and doors in the intercolumniations; of
the upper story, at least in late Hellenistic times,
a series of piers and large openings (fig. 8).
These spaces were probably provided with
double, or even triple doors, but might in all
likelihood be used on occasion for various sets
and other decorative features. The proskenion,
regularly eight feet or more in height, was no
doubt sometimes used as a logeion or stage.
Indeed, some scholars believe that it was regularly so used, though certain kinds of performances continued as in Hellenic times to be
presented in the orchestra. The type of scene-
building adopted in Italy (Pompeii) and Sicily
(Tyndaris, Segesta, Taormina, Syracuse, etc.)
resembled that at Athens. That is to say it was

a rectangular structure with projecting para-skenia. But whether the space between the wings was occupied by a proskenion and whether the whole building was more than one story in height are questions that are still in dispute.

The Roman theatre, on the other hand, like that of modern times was built upon level or nearly level ground and constituted an architectural unit. The portion designed for spectators, the *cavea,* was approximately a semi-circle and was supported by an imposing substructure containing passage-ways, staircases and landings with transverse lobbies leading to doors (*vomitoria*) which opened upon the diazomata or *praecinctiones* (figs. 15 and 16). At the top in many cases there was a covered gallery ornamented with columns and surmounted by supports for a huge awning of canvas (*velum, velarium*). Small theatres, like the smaller of the two at Pompeii and the Odeum of Herodes Atticus on the south-western slope of the Acropolis at Athens, were sometimes provided with a roof. The orchestra or pit, semi-circular like the cavea, was reserved for the use of senators and other officials and distinguished guests and in some instances (Pompeii (fig. 16), Timgad,

Dugga, etc.) had several low, broad steps on which to place the seats of honor. In lieu of the open parodi of the Hellenistic theatre were vaulted tunnels, their inner ends sometimes surmounted by level platforms (*tribunalia*) to serve as boxes for the magistrates and other dignitaries (figs. 15, 16 and 17).

Opposite the central part of the cavea was a wide and deep stage (*pulpitum*) not more than five feet in height with one or more short flights of steps leading into the orchestra. Its front wall might be either straight or broken into a series of niches and recesses variously adorned with pilasters and columns, while at its rear arose a lofty and irregular proscenium-wall as high as the uppermost rim of the cavea, sumptuously ornamented with columns, statues and the like, and having at least three doorways and near the top a sloping roof over the stage (fig. 17). The corner spaces flanking the stage were occupied by rooms, stairways and passages, while in the rear there was frequently a magnificent portico (fig. 15).

From these brief descriptions it is clear that in the process of modernization an Hellenistic theatre could not be converted into a Roman theatre of the pure type. A compromise form

was therefore adopted which involved three
fundamental changes: a deep stage was erected,
the wall at the rear was made higher and ornamented in conformity with the Roman style,
and with a few exceptions, as at Athens and
Priene, vaulted passageways replaced the open
parodi. In some theatres (Priene, Ephesus, etc.)
the stage was of the same height as the proskenion which it supplanted; in others (Athens,
Syracuse, the larger theatre at Pompeii, etc.) it
was made low like a Roman stage, but possibly
only as a result of a further reconstruction. On
this point agreement has not yet been reached.
Alterations affecting the auditorium were less
uniform in character. These might consist in the
erection of new seats of honor in the central part
of the auditorium on a level with the stage
(Priene), or in the construction of low steps in
the orchestra (Pompeii). In some cases, again,
as at Ephesus and at Corinth,[60] the lowest rows
of seats were removed and the orchestra converted into a pit. At Ephesus, too, tunnel-like
passages were cut through to the diazomata, and
similar entrances were obtained in other cases,
as at Pompeii and Taormina, by constructing
beyond the periphery of the earlier auditorium
a series of vaulted corridors with a gallery above

and doors opening upon the upper diazoma or praecinctio (fig. 16).

These few examples will suffice to give an idea of the various devices to which resort was had in the attempt to modernize the old style of building. It will be observed that in these reconstructed theatres the cavea, as also the orchestra, regularly exceeded a semi-circle and that the stage-building was relatively small (fig. 6). They occupy an intermediate position between the bipartite Hellenistic structure and the unified Roman theatre. Those having a relatively high stage (Priene, Ephesus, etc.) are sometimes designated Graeco-Roman. Perhaps it would not be improper to apply this name to all.

The Roman type of theatre which thus profoundly influenced the Hellenistic type was in origin itself an Hellenistic theatre modified to suit local needs and conditions. The chief modifying influence was the fact that from time immemorial the inhabitants of Italy had been accustomed to hold their dramatic performances, Atellan plays (p. 23), Phlyakes (p. 7) and the like, upon a stage. The Greek theatre, as we have seen, evolved from a circular orchestra with a primitive auditorium resting on a hill-slope. The scene-building, added only after many years, was in a sense fortuitous. The Roman theatre, on the other hand, developed from a rectangular stage with its various appurtenances; for a long period no attempt was made to secure an adequate auditorium. Indeed, so far as we know, two hundred years elapsed after the erection of the first stage in Rome in 364 B.C. for the Etruscan *ludiones* (p. 22) before a theatre was constructed in the city (·179 B.C.).[61] This was of wood and was built near the temple of Apollo. It was soon torn down, however, and time and again after this efforts were made to provide a suitable playhouse for Roman audiences only to meet with a similar fate. It was not until 55 B.C., three hundred years after the first stage had been erected, that Rome possessed a permanent stone theatre. This was built by Pompey near the Circus Flaminius, but even he, we are told,[62] in order to avoid censure for having erected a permanent theatre, added a temple of Venus Victrix at the top of the cavea so that the seats should appear to be but temple steps and the whole building was actually dedicated as a temple, not as a theatre! This was perhaps an unnecessary precaution. Yet only a century earlier (154 B.C.)

that stern old Roman P. Scipio Nasica had in-
duced the senate to order the destruction of
a stone theatre begun the year before, on
the ground that the presence of such a building would be injurious to public morals, and
to decree that henceforth no one should wish
to set seats for spectators or sit down himself at a theatrical performance, not only
in the city but within a mile of the city
gates! [63]

In the early days, then, only a scanty wooden
platform (*pulpitum*) with a structure at the
rear to serve as a scene-building (*scaena*) was
allowed. The place occupied by the spectators,
the *cavea* or " hollow," was without seats. During the lifetime of Plautus the space immediately in front of the pulpitum was reserved for
senators and other dignitaries.[64] Before the time
of Terence, however, the Romans had begun to
erect theatre-buildings, the earliest in 179 B.C.,
and after that for an entire century temporary
wooden theatres were erected year after year
for special occasions and then wastefully de-
molished. Some of these were of enormous size
and decorated with lavish extravagance. Most
splendid of all was that of the aedile M. Aemilius Scaurus (58 B.C.), of which the scaena was

three stories in height and adorned with three hundred sixty columns, three thousand statues, relief-plaques of glass and other rich trophies of his eastern campaigns.[65]

The cynical shrewdness of Pompey at length gave Rome a permanent theatre (55 B.C.). This was copied according to Plutarch [66] after the Hellenistic theatre at Mitylene (Lesbos), but was larger and more imposing. To what extent, however, the theatre of Pompey resembled its Hellenistic model is not known, and it is idle to attempt to reconstruct its original form. For the building was repeatedly restored and rebuilt, first by Augustus in 32 B.C. and then by Tiberius, Caligula, and many others, so that it became, if indeed it had not always been, a typical Roman theatre. Magnificently embellished with stucco and marble and adorned with numberless statues and columns it was always greatly admired and is frequently mentioned in ancient literature. Its seating capacity was perhaps ten thousand.

Two other permanent theatres were erected later, the one dedicated in 13 B.C. by L. Cornelius Balbus, friend of Pompey, Caesar, and Augustus, the other planned by Caesar but built by Augustus and dedicated in 13 B.C.

(Pliny [67] says 11 B.C.) to the memory of Marcellus, nephew and adopted son of Augustus, who died in 23 B.C. This theatre of Marcellus is near the Tiber, between it and the south-west end of the Capitoline, and is still one of the most impressive monuments of ancient Rome.

These three buildings — the only permanent theatres of Rome, unless one include also the small Odeum of Domitian (81–96 A.D.) — were built mostly of travertine or limestone, and the façade of the cavea consisted in each case of three series of arcades having attached half-columns, those of the lowest tier being Doric, of the second Ionic, of the uppermost Corinthian. Immediately within the piers of the first arcade there was an ambulatory that ran entirely round the semi-circular cavea, and the arrangement of walls, corridors, stairways and the like was very similar to that of the Colosseum.

Outside of Rome theatres of the Roman type were erected in many places, some small like the smaller theatres at Pompeii and Taormina, others large and sumptuously appointed, like that at Orange (fig. 18). Wherever found, whether in Italy or France or Greece or Asia

Minor (Aspendus, Termessus, Sagalassus, Perge) or Northern Africa (Timgad, Dugga) or far-away Syria (Gerasa), all alike bear witness to the amazing architectonic skill of the ancient Romans.

VIII. PROPERTIES; SCENES; MECHANICAL DEVICES

THE Greek theatre, as we have seen, evolved from a circular orchestra; the Roman began with a rectangular stage. This fundamental difference between the two species should never be lost to view. In the latter the stage accommodated actors and chorus, when there was a chorus; in the former chorus and actors at first occupied the orchestra. Even after the erection of a scene-building the orchestra-area continued to be used by actors as well as chorus throughout the remainder of the fifth century, probably until after the beginning of the Hellenistic period, possibly even until the Roman era. There is no incontestable evidence of a stage in the Greek theatre until at the earliest about 150 B.C., though it is only fair to state that some scholars believe that there was a low platform even as early as the fifth century and that the proskenion served as a stage from the time of its introduction. On these points unanimity of view may never be reached. But all

FIGURE 16. THE GRAECO-ROMAN THEATRE AT POMPEII

From a photograph by Alinari

are agreed that during the later centuries in theatres of the Hellenistic and Graeco-Roman
types non-dramatic choral performances and
perhaps also old dramas were rendered in the
orchestra, and ultimately also gladiatorial shows
and beast-baiting combats.

In the orchestra of the Greek theatre stood
an altar or *thymele* (p. 63), a word whose
meaning came in time to include the entire
orchestra-area. In the Roman period the name
thymele was sometimes applied to the stage.

The exact position of the altar is not certain.
In some theatres (Athens, Epidaurus) it appears to have occupied the middle point of the
orchestra. At Priene however it stood at the
periphery opposite the centre of the proskenion
(fig. 6), and this position may have been of
common occurrence.

The thymele may be regarded as a part of
the theatre itself. It was permanent, not temporary. Other altars might of course be introduced
as needed along with all the various accessories,
tombs, statues, seats, couches, drapes, rugs,
screens, shrubbery and the like, required for the
sets of the different plays. But in the earliest
times both in Greece and Rome such properties
were doubtless of the most meagre sort.

At first there was no scenery. At the time of its introduction (p. 75) and for long afterward scene-painting must have been of a simple, conventional sort. Perhaps it was not scene-painting at all in the modern sense of the term, but merely adornment of the scene-building. However this may be, certainly the art of Agatharchus (p. 76) was not realistic. In the fifth century B.C. the Greeks had nothing comparable to our modern illusionistic painting. True, in the *Ion* (*c.* 412 B.C.) of Euripides, the scene of which is laid before the temple of Apollo at Delphi, the chorus in a long passage (*vss.* 184–218) admire the sculptures that adorn the shrine. There is Heracles with golden scimiter slaying the Lernaean hydra, Iolaus " uplifting a flame-wrapped torch."

> *Lo, lo, this other behold*
> *Who rideth a winged horse, dealing death*
> *To a dragon that vomiteth fiery breath,*
> *   A monster of shape threefold.*
> *O yea, mine eyes turn swiftly on all . . .*
> *But O, see there on the marble wall*
> *   The battle rout of the giant horde!* [68]

Quite unwarranted however is the assumption that this passage affords evidence of elaborate

and even realistic scene-painting in the days of
Euripides. In so vast a theatre minutiae of composition would be lost upon the unaided eye.
Like the seashore in the *Philoctetes*, the darkness and mud in the *Frogs*, the brilliant stars in
the *Rhesus*, and the moonlight in the *Merchant
of Venice*, these adornments in the *Ion* were no
doubt left to the imagination.

> *And yet, no less, the audience there*
> *Thrilled through all changes of Despair,*
> *Hope, Anger, Fear, Delight, and Doubt.*

> .　　.　　.　　.　　.　　.

> *This is the Actor's gift: to share*
> *All moods, all passions, nor to care*
> *One whit for scene, so he without*
> *Can lead men's minds the roundabout.*[69]

But before the close of the Hellenistic era the
art of the scene-painter had made great progress
and during the Roman period attained a high
degree of realism especially in the representation of architectural features. What it was like
may be seen in the numerous wall-paintings of
Pompeii.[70] At Rome such decoration of the
scaena by means of painting was introduced as
late as the year 99 B.C. by the aedile Claudius

Pulcher. About the same time a certain Apaturius painted the back-scene of a theatre at Tralles in Caria, depicting " columns and statues, centaurs supporting the architraves, rotundas with round roofs on them, pediments with overhanging returns and cornices ornamented with lions' heads . . . and then on top of it all he made an episcaenium in which were painted rotundas, porticoes, half-pediments, and all the different kinds of decoration employed in a roof." [71] The small theatre at Pompeii (c. 80 B.C.) was similarly adorned. This style of ornamentation was very likely the forerunner of the use of actual columns, statues and the like as in the theatres of M. Aemilius Scaurus and Pompey (p. 95).

The settings for plays both Greek and Roman may be divided roughly into four classes. In the first of these there is either no back-scene, as in the *Suppliants* of Aeschylus and perhaps also in his *Persians,* or, if present, it is not used for entrances and exits, but represents a hill or other eminence, or else is entirely ignored. Thus for the *Oedipus Coloneus* of Sophocles the setting is a sacred grove; for the fragmentary *Andromeda* of Euripides, a cliff bordering on the sea. In the second type the scene is a stretch of

FIGURE 17. THE STAGE AND *SCAENAE FRONS* OF THE
ROMAN THEATRE AT ASPENDUS

After a restoration by Niemann, published in Lanckoroński, *Städte Pamphyliens*

wild country with rocks, trees and bushes, and
a single entrance at the rear representing the
mouth of a cavern or hollow rock, as in the
Cyclops of Euripides, the *Birds* of Aristophanes,
and the *Philoctetes* of Sophocles. In the last the
orchestra is imagined to be the shore of Lem-
nos; the background, a desolate hillside with a
grotto part way up the slope to which a path
leads from the beach below.[72] In the third class
the skene represents a building: a palace, a
temple, a house, a hut, and the like, as occasion
demands. Usually in such cases only one door in
the back-scene is required. In a few instances,
however, two doors are so used, and occasionally even three. Examples are the *Agamemnon*
of Aeschylus, the *Alcestis* of Euripides, the
Wasps of Aristophanes, and many others.
Lastly the set is a series of houses or other structures, two or three in number ranged side by
side, as in the *Andromache* of Euripides, the
Clouds of Aristophanes, the *Epitrepontes* of
Menander, and the *Andria* of Terence.

In general the range of choice appears to have
been greater in the fifth century B.C. than in the
third and later centuries. This impression may
be due however to defective evidence. Certainly quite stereotyped is the setting required

by most of the extant comedies of Menander, Plautus, and Terence: two houses facing upon a street. Some of the Roman plays, as the *Phormio* (*vs.* 891) and the *Eunuchus* (*vs.* 845), require also a narrow alley (*angiportum*) leading back from the street between the houses or at one side. This might be used for entrances and exits or as a place of concealment. Very likely it was of Hellenistic origin.

The entrances at the sides, the parodi of the Menandrian theatre, the doors at the ends of the stage in the Roman theatre, are said to have had a conventional significance. The ancient notices regarding the convention are confused and in part corrupt, so that the details are not entirely clear. But it is usually stated in the following form: the entrance on the left of the actor was supposed to lead to the centre of the city (the market-place or forum), or to the city as a whole in case the setting was rural; that on the right, to the harbor or the country. According to another interpretation the city and the harbor both lay in the same direction. Whatever the truth in the matter, the convention originated at Athens and arose from the situation of the theatre of Dionysus. But it was not in vogue in the fifth century B.C., though traces of it are already discernible in the last two extant comedies of Aristophanes: the *Ecclesiazusae* (392 B.C.) and the *Plutus* (388 B.C.).[73]

Changes of the set during the progress of a play were of rare occurrence; changes of the scene or locality, frequent. Of the latter the greater number were facilitated by the use of a multiple set, or else depended merely upon the suggestiveness of word and action and the visualizing power of the imagination which schools both the poet's pen and the apprehending mind to give

> *to airy nothing*
> A *local habitation and a name.*[74]

Thus in the *Frogs* of Aristophanes the orchestra represents at first the road and an open space before the house of Heracles. Suddenly Charon, grim ferryman of the dead, appears rowing his tiny boat, and in a twinkling the orchestra becomes a lake. The presence of the boat and Dionysus' exclamation " Why, that's a lake, by Zeus! " are alone sufficient to whisk the imagination of the audience to the Acherusian shores. With the disappearance of Charon and his boat the lake is forgotten, and the orchestra becomes in turn the regions of the dead, dark and loathsome. Again the poet waves his wand, and darkness and mud give place to light most beautiful, and verdant meadows and groves of glossy myrtle, where the blessed " initiates " dance and sing in joyous revelry. Another shift, and Dionysus and his slave stand at the portals of Pluto's dwelling. Similar imagined changes of scene occur in many dramas, more particularly in the older period.

Whenever the setting was altered between plays or within plays, as in the *Eumenides* of Aeschylus and the *Ajax* of Sophocles, this was done in the case of the Greek theatre in full view of the audience. There was no curtain, nor is there the slightest trustworthy evidence for the use of flats. But from about 100 B.C. the Roman theatre apparently had both. The curtain (*aulaeum*) was rolled about a cylinder in a slot or deep recess which extended across the front of the stage (it is shown clearly in fig. 16) and was therefore drawn up (*tollere*) at the end of the play and lowered (*mittere*) at the beginning. Thus Cicero in his defence of Caelius, who was accused of having attempted to poison the infamous Clodia, exclaims: [75] " This then is the end not of a real drama but of a farce, in which when there is no conclusion some one makes his

escape, the clappers clash, the curtain is raised."
Horace complaining of the degraded taste of the
audiences of his day says: [76] " For four hours
or more the curtain is kept down (*aulaea pre-
muntur*) while squadrons of horse and bodies
of foot are seen flying; presently there passes
the spectacle of unfortunate kings dragged with
hands behind their backs; chariots of every
kind and shape hurry along." The aulaeum was
adorned with figures which, as the curtain rose,
seemed to be drawing it up after them as is clear
from Virgil:

> *and inwoven there*
> See *painted Britons the purple tapestry-folds*
> *upbear.*[77]

In this passage the poet adds: " see the stage
dispart as the scenes swing round " (*vel scaena
ut versis discedat frontibus*). This is a reference to two methods of indicating a change of
scene on the Roman stage. The one consisted in
shifting painted screens (*scaena ductilis*) comparable to modern flats; the other, according to
one opinion, in turning about a pivot screens or
panels having pictures on both sides (*frontes*),
a device known as a *scaena versilis*. It is usually
however differently explained and identified

with certain revolving prisms (*periacti*) mentioned by several late writers and described by
Vitruvius: " triangular pieces of machinery
(Δ, Δ) which revolve, each having three
decorated faces. When the play is to be changed,
or when gods enter to the accompaniment of
sudden claps of thunder, these may be revolved
and present a face differently decorated." [78]
But the identification is not certain and it seems
better to hold that the periacti constituted a
third means of altering the scene. They stood
at the two ends of the stage. When the periacti
were introduced is not known. There is no evidence that they were in use before Hellenistic
or even Roman times, though one ancient gram-
marian ascribes their invention to Aeschylus. [79]

In an amusing passage in one of the early
comedies of Aristophanes, the *Acharnians* (425
B.C.), the leading character, Dicaeopolis, comes
to the house of the tragic poet Euripides and as
he pounds upon the door calls in a loud voice:
" Euripides, dear Rippy! Answer my summons,
if ever you answered any man! 'Tis I, Dicaeopolis of Cripplegate! " From within comes the
response: " But I'm not at leisure." " At least
be wheeled out! " shouts back Dicaeopolis.
" Well," replies Euripides, " I'll have myself

wheeled out " (*vss.* 403 ff.). Thereupon the doors are thrown open and the poet is wheeled out apparently reclining on a couch. The ensuing dialogue, one of the most diverting in all the pages of Aristophanes, Euripides brings to an abrupt end with the remark: " The fellow is insolent; shut the door! " (*vs.* 479). There is a similar scene in the *Thesmophoriazusae* (*c.* 411 B.C.), except that in this case the tragic poet Agathon is the butt of the fun, though Euripides, who is present, is himself also held up to ridicule. Agathon suddenly terminates the scene with the command: " Let some one wheel me in at once! " (*vss.* 95 ff., 265).

In these two passages Aristophanes employs with comic effect a contrivance used in the Greek theatre to disclose interior scenes, and known as an *eccyclema,* " that which is rolled out," or *exostra,* " that which is thrust forth." The ancient descriptions of this curious device are confused.[80] It is sometimes spoken of in such a way as to suggest a wheeled platform which could be pushed out through a door; at other times it is referred to as a wheeled and *revolving* platform. More than this we do not know, except that it was used by Aristophanes to heighten his ridicule of Euripides. Naturally modern opinion is divided. Some believe that the eccyclema was a semi-circular platform attached to a portion of the front wall of the scene-building and the whole revolved about a pivot after the manner of a butterfly valve; others, that it was a trundle-platform. A third view is that both types were used, the former until about 430 B.C., the latter during the closing decades of the fifth century and later.[81] Equally divergent are the theories regarding the extent to which the eccyclema was employed. The extreme conservatives accepting the statements of the scholiasts assume its general use by Aeschylus and Sophocles as well as by Euripides and Aristophanes, not to mention the host of poets whose plays have been lost. The extreme radicals, on the other hand, deny the credibility of the scholia and reject the eccyclema except when the evidence in its favor is overwhelming. Between these two positions there is every shade of opinion.

Whatever the truth in the matter, the need of such a contrivance singularly emphasizes for us the limitations of the Greek theatre. In the lack of suitable arrangements for showing interiors the playwrights were compelled to present imaginary interiors out of doors. The effect

FIGURE 18. THE ROMAN THEATRE AT ORANGE

From a Neuerdein photograph

must have been much the same as that on the Elizabethan stage when various articles of furniture were brought out to suggest an inner scene as is indicated by such stage directions as " a bed thrust out," " enter Elizabeth in her bed," etc.[82] The audience of Shakespeare, like that of Euripides, doubtless accepted the convention with entire complaisance.

There was however another and more natural way of suggesting inner scenes which appears to have been extensively employed both in the Greek and Roman theatres. This was by means of a *prothyron* or portico (Latin *vestibulum*). The opening scene of the *Orestes* of Euripides shows us Electra at the bedside of her brother who has been desperately ill for five days. Similarly in the *Clouds* of Aristophanes (*vss.* 1 ff.) Strepsiades is lying on his couch trying to sleep. Nearby snores Phidippides under a mountain of blankets; the servants too are snoring. It is night time; the lamp sputters and goes out. These are plainly bedroom scenes, yet they are staged out of doors, apparently in the portico. Many other examples occur in the dramas of the fifth century.

In the plays of Plautus and Terence, too, all borrowed from New Comedy, the vestibule fre-

quently serves in lieu of an inner room. Thus in
the *Asinaria* of Plautus (*vss.* 830 ff.) a banquet
is in progress before the door of a procuress,
Cleaereta. Argyrippus and his father Demaene-
tus, who shares his couch with the courtesan
Philaenium, are carousing, when in rushes the
old man's wife and drags him from the house of
vice. A similar scene is found in Plautus' *Stichus*
(*vss.* 683 ff.). Two slaves, Stichus and Sanga-
rinus, celebrate a feast with a girl, Stephanium,
before the house of Pamphilus. In the *Mostel-
laria* (*vss.* 157 ff.) the courtesan Philematium
enters with her maid, Scapha, who has a mirror
and a box containing toilet articles. As Philematium makes her toilet Philolaches saunters
up and watches the proceedings with manifest
interest.

Innumerable are the passages both in Greek
and Roman drama in which the action takes
place " before the door," " in the portico,"
" *ante aedes*," " *ante januam*," " *ante ostium*,"
though not in all are interior scenes so clearly
indicated as in those which have been cited.[83]
How the portico was represented is not known.
In the period when the proskenion was in use as
a background the removal of a few panels from
between the columns probably sufficed.

In addition to the various mechanical devices which have been described many others were in use in the ancient theatre. Their names and descriptions may be found in the larger treatises. The chief ancient authority is the lexicographer Pollux of the second century A.D.[84] But unfortunately his meaning is not always clear, he often exhibits a most exasperating indifference to chronological sequence, and not infrequently converts a specific instance into a general practice. In spite of these defects, however, his book is of great value and, as we shall see (p. 150), exercised a considerable influence upon the theatre during the period of the Renaissance. He speaks of subterranean stairs, which he calls Charonian steps, for the use of ghosts and other apparitions, trap-doors, devices for imitating thunder and lightning, the eccyclema, and several other contrivances, among them the " machine."

The machine, known also as the " crane," was an arrangement by means of which actors could be suspended in the air or lifted to the upper part of the scene-building or lowered from a height to the level of the orchestra or swept across the scene. Thus in the *Peace* of Aristophanes Trygaeus straddles a huge dung-beetle and flies upward to the abode of Zeus. In the lost *Bellerophon* of Euripides the hero, we are told, mounted from earth to heaven on the back of the winged steed Pegasus. In the *Clouds* of Aristophanes Socrates is discovered suspended in a basket, and with mock profundity announces: "I tread the air and contemplate the sun." The contrivance employed in these and similar scenes is said to have been placed at one side high up above the skene,[85] but as to the manner in which it was operated there is no definite information. Probably it resembled an ordinary crane.

The date when the machine was added to the appurtenances of the theatre is not known. Some ascribe it to Euripides; others quite as confidently to Aeschylus. That, however, it was often employed by Euripides and Aristophanes is beyond question, especially by the former for introducing a god at the close of a play to make an epilogic pronouncement — a feature imitated by Seneca in his *Hercules Oetaeus* and often, though usually in a somewhat different manner, by Renaissance playwrights (p. 176) — or to untangle a situation that has become too intricate. From its frequent use for the latter purpose particularly by inferior dramatists

FIGURE 19. ACTORS IN OLD COMEDY
From a photograph of the Museum at Würzburg

arose the familiar expression "a god from the machine" (*deus ex machina*). An interesting parallel to this is found in the French *Les Miracles de Notre Dame* and the German *Marienspiele,* in which time and time again the Blessed Virgin appears to rescue a favorite from some dire predicament. Parallels occur also in the drama of modern times. Molière's *Tartuffe* is a case in point. Orgon, helplessly entangled in a web of intrigue, is set free at last in the name of the king by an officer of the police.[86]

IX. THE CHORUS AND SPECTACLE

THE vast size of the theatre at Athens and the fact that performances were held under the open sky exercised a profound influence not only upon the character of Athenian drama but also upon the manner of its presentation.[87] The broad and simple themes of tragedy were presented with a certain largeness and massiveness of effect which would never have been imparted to them had the Greek theatre resembled a modern playhouse or even the semi-mediaeval " Swan " or " Globe " of Shakespeare's day. Greek tragic drama was not composed for a cramped stage and artificial lights, but for a large arena and the brilliant sunshine of a southern clime; and the same was true also of satyr-play and comedy, particularly fifth-century comedy. New Comedy shows the influence of the theatre to a less degree. It was better adapted to presentation on a comparatively small stage, and in this respect as in several others was an anticipation of modern drama.

Of even greater importance than the influence of the theatre in determining the form and character of Greek drama was that of its choral origin. In the case of tragedy the choral element was predominant in the Thespian and early Aeschylean periods and until at least the close of the fifth century continued to be an integral part of the play. The singing of the odes was accompanied by rhythmic movements characterized by dignity and grace, a form of dance called by the Greeks *emmeleia*, "harmony," to which however the word "dance" with its modern connotations seems singularly inappropriate. When the songs expressed excitement steps and gestures naturally were quickened. An ode of ecstatic joy might be attended by a lively mimetic dance known as an *hyporcheme* ("dance-song") of which no finer example occurs than that in the *Oedipus Tyrannus* of Sophocles (1086 ff.) where it relieves the tragic tension just before the climax of this heart-rending play.

The choral odes, with the exception of that sung as the choreutae entered the orchestra or immediately thereafter, went by the name of *stasima* (singular *stasimon*). The entrance-song was known as a *parodos;* a lyrical dialogue between an actor and the chorus, as a *kommos*. If any part of the play preceded the parodos it was designated a prologue; the concluding portion, *exodos;* while all that came between two choral songs was called an *episode*, "an additional portion," a word which records an important phase in the development of the drama. For in the Thespian play the speeches of the actor and the dialogues in which he engaged were looked upon as interruptions, interludes. The term, once established, continued to be employed even after the relationship had been completely reversed and the choral songs themselves had become in turn the interludes.

The beginning of the change in this relationship came very early. Indeed, no sooner were the acted episodes linked up into a connected plot than the stasima began to partake of the nature of intermissions. This is clear from the fact that during the singing of a stasimon any amount of time — hours, days, weeks, even years — might be imagined to elapse. This is one of the most important conventions of Greek drama.

In addition to the choral odes there occurred also not infrequently, especially in the plays of Euripides, solos (monodies) by actors and even duets and trios in which the chorus did not participate. These duets and trios might be wholly lyrical in form or might consist of song alternating with speech or with verses declaimed to musical accompaniment somewhat after the manner of the *recitativo* or *musica parlante* of the seventeenth century.

So prominent, indeed, was song and lyrical declamation in Greek drama of the fifth century, comedy as well as tragedy, that some have seen therein a similarity to modern opera. But the comparison should not be pressed; in most respects the two are quite distinct, though one must admit that in the case of the miscalled *opéra comique* or the German *Singspiel,* in which spoken dialogue alternates with song, there is a certain superficial resemblance. And in this connection one should remember too that the attempt to reproduce the musical declamation of ancient tragedy was the immediate generative impulse which led to the birth of opera (p. 181).

The manner in which the choreutae entered the orchestra varied widely. Sometimes it was a formal march by " ranks " and " files " to the accompaniment of the anapaestic chant, followed by an ode consisting, as in the case of a stasimon, of a series of stanzas arranged in pairs (strophes, antistrophes). Or the chorus might enter in silence, then sing an ode as in the previous case, or engage in a lyrical dialogue with an actor. In some instances the choreutae entered singly or in irregular groups, as in the *Seven against Thebes* of Aeschylus and the *Oedipus at Colonus* of Sophocles. In the fifth century at least there was no hard and fast rule. As to the size of the tragic chorus, Aeschylus we are told employed normally twelve performers; Sophocles and Euripides, fifteen.

Satyr-drama was structurally similar to tragedy upon which it had been modeled, but the satyric dance (*sikinnis*) was less dignified than the usual tragic dance and the movements more vigorous.

Old Comedy differed from the other types in many particulars. It was far more complex in structure and exhibited certain features peculiar to itself such as the *agon* or contest and the *parabasis* or address to the audience. But it resembled the other species in point of lyrical character. The chorus consisted of twenty-four performers often divided into two equal groups each with a leader. The comic dance, violent, unrestrained, even obscene at times, was called a *kordax,* and the dances and songs of the chorus were almost as prominent as the purely dramatic portions. The scenes were often crowded, the action brisk and diversified; and in this action the choreutae might participate with as much freedom and vigor as any of the actors themselves.

Before the death of Aristophanes (*c.* 386 B.C.) lyrical exuberance departed from comedy, the chorus lost its dramatic character and soon thereafter passed into its senescence. In the plays of Menander it appears in its senility rendering pitiful *entr'acte* entertainment of dance and song; in the next century it died. The extant comedies of Plautus and Terence contain no choruses except for a brief and unimportant appearance of a band of fishermen in the *Rudens.*[88]

The chorus died, but the singing of monodies lived on. Possibly this too languished for a season; the evidence is defective. But at any rate in Roman comedy, especially Plautine comedy, actors' solos and the declaiming of passages to musical accompaniment, both known as *cantica,* played a large and important rôle. The instrument employed in all such cases was the *tibia* or clarinet.[2] Frequently, no doubt, instrumental music filled the pauses in the action. A clear case in point is in the *Pseudolus* of Plautus. As he leaves the stage at the close of the second " act " Pseudolus remarks: " Meanwhile the pipe-player (*tibicen*) here will entertain you."

In comedy the choral element early began to atrophy and ultimately disappeared; in tragedy, on the other hand, as also no doubt in satyr-drama, the chorus appears to have been retained as long as these two types of plays continued in vogue. In the earliest period it was an integral part of the play, and this appears to have been true to a certain extent also of the tragedies of the Roman poets Ennius (239–169 B.C.), Pacuvius (220–*c*. 130 B.C.), and Accius (170–84? B.C.), of whom Ennius was most like Euripides and Accius like Aeschylus.[89] But probably during the two centuries from the death of Euripides (406 B.C.) to the time of Ennius the chorus was not always so important a feature of tragic drama. Even if it regularly engaged freely in the action (and as to this we cannot be certain), its songs were often merely irrelevant interludes such as we noticed in the case of New Comedy — an innovation said to have been introduced by the poet Agathon who flourished about the end of the fifth century B.C., and a condition of affairs well illustrated by the florid, rhetorical dramas of the younger Seneca (born 3 A.D.).

In Seneca's plays there are regularly four such intermezzi; and as a result, five acts. In this particular, as doubtless in many others, Seneca's practice reflects the decadent drama of the Hellenistic era. And back of this in turn lay the influence of Euripides, several of whose plays exhibit the same peculiarity. Hence Horace, who derived his theory of the poetic art in large part from Alexandrian critics, proclaimed the rule: [90]

Neve *minor neu sit quinto productior actu*
Fabula, quae posci volt et spectata reponi

Five acts a play must have, nor more nor less
To keep the stage and have a marked success.

How Horace and Seneca influenced modern dramatic theory and practice will be briefly discussed in our concluding chapter.

In Roman tragedy, to judge from the extant fragments and from the perfervid chamber-plays of Seneca, the chorus did not as a rule remain on the scene continually from its entrance to the close. " Except for its songs between the acts, it was much like the mobs, retinues and armies on the modern stage, though it had a more intimate part in the action." " It probably came and went as it was needed, thus adding life and movement." [91] This dramatic device occurred also in Greek drama, though perhaps not to the same extent. Several instances dating even from the fifth century B.C. are known, as in the *Eumenides* of Aeschylus, the *Ajax* of Sophocles, and in the *Alcestis* and the *Helena* of Euripides. Other examples are found in the *Ecclesiazusae* (392 or 389 B.C.) of Aristophanes, in the *Rhesus*, a stirring play of uncertain authorship, but commonly assigned to the fourth century B.C.,[92] and, as has already been noticed, in comedies of the Menandrian period.

It is interesting to note, further, that sometimes (how often we do not know) advantage was taken of the absence of the chorus to change the setting. Thus in the *Eumenides*, while the chorus was gone in pursuit of the hapless Orestes, the scene-shifters removed the omphalos and other symbols of the temple of Apollo at Delphi and substituted therefor a statue of Athena to indicate an ancient shrine at Athens. A change of scene, possibly of the setting as well, occurred also in the *Ajax* of Sophocles while the chorus was off stage.

The leader of the chorus (*coryphaeus,* "head-man"), at least in tragedy of the fifth century and in Old Comedy, had a rôle of great responsibility. Not only did he lead the chanting of the anapaestic march of the parodos and the singing of the choral lyrics; he was also leader of the dances, sometimes quite intricate, which accompanied these songs; frequently delivered passages in recitative; and in addition to all this participated more or less freely in the dialogue of the episodes. Evidently the success of a performance, particularly in the early period when the lyrical element was of preponderating significance, depended in no slight degree upon the ability of the person selected for this important rôle. It may seem a bit surprising therefore that in the official records of dramatic victories the names of the coryphaei were not included. The reason for the omission was the fact that a contest of chorus-leaders was never instituted. Though his task was arduous and his position in the troupe one of pivotal importance, the coryphaeus was held in lower honor than the protagonist.

In the Roman theatre, as has been noticed,

chorus and actors occupied the stage; in the
Greek theatre, in the fifth century at least, the
orchestra-area. Both arrangements made possible the easy commingling of the various participants, the formation of mobile, animated
groups, whose life-like character was further
enhanced by the presence of attendants,
soldiers, citizens and others as the occasion
might demand; and the spectacle thus presented
was sometimes very impressive. Thus in the
Suppliants of Aeschylus the daughters of Dan-
aus and their hand-maidens struggle in terror
against the attacks of the herald and his attendants, who seize the girls by the hair and
are about to drag them to the ship when the
king enters with his bodyguard and puts an end
to the strife; in the *Seven against Thebes* the
king Eteocles addresses the crowd of soldiers
and other citizens, urging them to show themselves men and defend their beleaguered city;
in the *Agamemnon* the chorus of elders draw
their swords and advance to engage in battle
with Aegisthus and his bodyguard; and earlier
in the same play there is the triumphal return
of Agamemnon with chariots, soldiers, captives,
and booty-bearers.

Sometimes the effect was absolutely overpowering, as when in the *Eumenides* of Aeschylus the Furies with their black robes, snaky locks and repulsive features burst from the shrine of Apollo and joined in a hymn and dance of fiendish rage before the temple doors. The sight was so terrifying, we are told,[93] that children fainted and women miscarried; no doubt an exaggeration, but even so a story that bears faithful testimony to the gripping power of this stupendous scene.

In general, however, the Greek playwrights of the best period kept action and spectacle and all other aspects of realism well within bounds. The rule " Nothing too much " they observed with scrupulous care.

But among the Romans the case was different. The Roman delighted in realism. Witness the portrait busts and sculptured reliefs, witness the cruel gladiatorial combats, the mimic sea-fights, the disgustingly merciless beast-baitings. Amid conditions such as these things suggest even comedy, boisterous, rollicking, laughter-provoking comedy, had a struggle to maintain itself. Tragic drama was in a more desperate case. If the latter was to hold its own in competition with the brutal shows so dear to the heart of the Roman populace, how could it eschew realistic spectacle? It could not, and it did not. In the best period, indeed, the period of "the great Roman trinity," Ennius, Pacuvius, and Accius, such effects were held in leash; excesses were avoided. But after the death of Accius (84? B.C.) taste became depraved, "the stage was swamped in magnificent pageantry." [94] The passion for spectacle was indulged without restraint. For hours at a time the progress of a play might be delayed while captives in chains were haled across the stage, chariots rumbled by, horses and mules passed in endless procession. Even battles were staged for the delectation of the applauding multitudes. The damaging effect of all this upon dramatic art can readily be imagined. The six hundred mules introduced into the *Clytemnestra* of Accius (p. 19) on the occasion of the dedication of Pompey's theatre (55 B.C.) make a sorry contrast with the two chariots and the groups of soldiers, captives and booty-bearers in the *Agamemnon* of Aeschylus or with the modest, though stately, procession which brings the *Eumenides* to a close.

X. ACTORS AND ACTING; COSTUMES

AMONG the Greeks the common word for actor was *hypocrites* (ὑποκριτής; whence English "hypocrite"); among the Romans, *histrio*. Each records an event of large significance in the history of ancient drama. The former, which in this connection meant "answerer," that is, one who made reply to the chorus, carries us back to the days of Thespis, when, as will be recalled, there was but a single actor, and dialogue was therefore impossible except as the chorus, represented by the coryphaeus, participated. The latter, a Latinized form of the Etruscan *ister*, "a dancer," reminds us that the story of the theatre at Rome begins with the introduction of *ludiones* from Etruria to stay the ravages of a fearful pestilence.

In time other words also came into use, as *actor* ("manager," "actor-manager") among the Romans; among the Greeks, τραγῳδός (tragoedus) and κωμῳδός (comoedus), old

terms both of them (p. 14), whose meanings by
a natural differentiation and selection gradually narrowed down to leading actor or protagonist in the fields of tragedy and comedy
respectively. The members of the Dionysiac guilds were known as " The Artists of
Dionysus " or " The Dionysiac Artists," or
sometimes when the meaning was otherwise
perfectly clear merely as " The Artists " par
excellence.

The history of these guilds is a matter of considerable interest. At first the dramatic poets
presented their plays in person, as did Thespis
and also Aeschylus at the beginning of his
career, but after the introduction of a second
actor the art of acting quickly became professional and by the middle of the fifth century
was sufficiently advanced for contests between
eminent actors to be established (449 B.C.), and
some fifty or sixty years later after the deaths
of Euripides (406), Sophocles (406/5), and
Aristophanes (386) became so highly developed
that it overshadowed even that of the dramatic
author himself. " An age of great actors succeeded to an age of great poets." [95] It was at
this time (early fourth century B.C.) that the
Actors' Guild was established at Athens, an

FIGURE 20. GREEK TRAGIC ACTOR'S
COSTUME

From the Andromeda-*krater* found at Capua, now in Berlin.
Date about 400 B.C.

organization which included all members of the
musical and theatrical professions: poets, actors, singers, trainers, and musicians. This guild
became very powerful, and as contests in music
and the drama were regarded as religious functions its members enjoyed many privileges and
immunities not accorded the ordinary citizen,
such as exemption from naval and military service and freedom of travel from state to state
even in time of war. For these reasons prominent actors were not infrequently employed as
negotiators of peace between hostile states and
were sent on other important missions of inter-
national significance.

In the course of time other organizations similar to that of Athens were formed in many
different communities, until ultimately the Artists of Dionysus were bound together in strong
and influential unions throughout the Greek-
speaking world. The more eminent members of
the profession were sought after by princes and
kings and were generously rewarded for their
services. Some members were of course poor
artists, some even of low character, but the profession itself was not regarded as in any way
derogatory to one's social position. The art of
acting was an honorable calling.

Among the Romans the case was almost totally different.[96] The *histriones* who as has been noted were regularly of foreign extraction, some freedmen, the majority slaves, were as a rule despised and rated on a level with thieves, panderers, cut-throats and gladiators. Flogging was a common form of punishment; the pay received (*lucar*) was usually pitifully small. If a citizen became an actor, he suffered the curtailment of his civic privileges: he became *infamis*. Amateurs, however, might perform in *Atellanae* (p. 23) without loss of citizenship or social prestige, and occasionally even a professional actor of exceptional ability might extricate himself from the mire of opprobrium and rise to an honorable standing in the community. Brilliant examples were the comedian Q. Roscius (died about 62 B.C.) upon whom Sulla conferred the golden ring of the equestrian order and whom Cicero admired and befriended, and his contemporary, the tragedian Clodius Aesopus (died 54 B.C.). These were the last great actors of Rome. Both, contrary to the usual course, amassed vast fortunes; both trained pupils in the art of acting, and with such success that the influence of their schools outlasted the Republic. The technique of Roscius in particular was so finished that his name came to signify in any craft or art the acme of perfection.

In the time of the Empire the status of actors appears to have been somewhat improved. But in spite of all, the lot of the professional entertainers, recruited as they were from the lowest orders and branded with the stigma of *infamia,* continued to be an unenviable one. A few might bask in the sunshine of imperial or magisterial favor; the majority were despised and denounced as moral lepers, outcasts from society. Long after the breaking up of the Empire this attitude of aversion persisted. Indeed, it may even be that the prejudice which still exists in certain circles toward the acting profession harks back to the days of Rome.

In tragic drama the number of actors, who in addition to the coryphaeus had speaking parts in a single scene or in two consecutive scenes, ordinarily did not exceed three, though four were sometimes so employed, as in the *Andromache* of Euripides where Peleus enters (*vs.* 547) to a group of three actors, one of whom however is a child, and in the *Agamemnon, Troades, Hercules* and *Oedipus* of Seneca. Four actors were apparently required also in the *Oedipus at Colonus* of Sophocles. If only three were employed, the rôle of Theseus must have been assumed by each of the three in turn, a possible but very unnatural arrangement. The rule, as usually stated, that the Greek playwrights were restricted to the use of three actors only is open to question and in recent years has been vigorously challenged.[97] As a matter of fact, however, most of the extant Greek tragedies, if masks be employed, as they were in ancient times, do not require more than three actors; and the occasional awkward silence of a fourth person who though addressed does not reply, as Pylades in the *Orestes* of Euripides (*vss.* 1591 ff.), who says not a word in spite of the ardent appeal of Menelaus, is difficult to explain on any other supposition than that for some reason the poet had only three actors at his disposal. Yet this may not be the correct explanation; perhaps no such limitation was imposed in connection with the dramatic festivals at Athens either during the fifth century or later. But the case of the strolling troupes of actors which toured Attica and other parts of Greece and gave exhibitions of plays for pay, a practice which began probably before the close of the fifth century, was different. For reasons of economy such traveling companies of performers were in all probability reduced to the lowest possible number, and from this practice may have arisen the custom of limiting the actors to three. But that this was ever formulated as a rigid *rule* cannot be proved and appears to be very improbable.

But whatever the truth in the matter as concerns tragedy, comedy appears not to have any such restriction. In the plays of Aristophanes there are several passages in which four actors have speaking parts, while the comedies of Plautus and Terence contain many scenes or groups of consecutive scenes in which four and even five different persons engage in the dialogue. Some plays may have required as many as seven actors. But of course the number of *characters* in a play, whether comedy or tragedy, often far exceeded the number of the performers who had speaking parts. In the extant dramas they vary from three in the *Suppliants* of Aeschylus, the earliest of all the plays which have been preserved, to at least twenty-three in the *Birds* of Aristophanes. Without doubt therefore rôles were frequently doubled, a practice still in vogue to a limited extent. In antiquity it must have been of very common occurrence. Until late Roman times the performers, whether actors, choreutae, or mutes, were regularly men or boys, except in mimes and pantomimes (p. 26 ff.).

In writings of late date one meets occasionally with the term *protagonist* ("chief contestant") applied specifically to the leading actor in a play. The word may have been so used also in the fifth and fourth centuries B.C., but there is no certain evidence that this was the case. Another term, *deuteragonist* ("second, or assistant contestant"), also employed in modern treatises, is of very rare occurrence in ancient documents and with one exception is, like protagonist, found only in writings of the post-classical period. The exception is a speech of Demosthenes dating from the middle of the fourth century in which a certain Ischander is said to be deuteragonist to the orator Aeschines and to assist him in forwarding his designs.[98] Although Ischander was a tragic actor, as was also Aeschines on occasion, this passage is not in itself sufficient to prove that the word deuteragonist had already acquired the meaning "second actor" which it bore in late times, as the passage in question refers to political activities. So in the case of the term *tritagonist* ("third contestant"). Again and again in the speeches

of Demosthenes, by whom perhaps it was invented, this word is applied to his rival Aeschines and always as a term of ridicule and re-
proach with the meaning " a third-rate actor."
There is no evidence that it ever became a
recognized title. Because of the uncertainty,
therefore, that attaches to these two terms,
deuteragonist and tritagonist, it would be better
not to use them in discussing the theatrical conventions and practices of the ancients.

The costumes employed in each of the several
species of dramatic entertainment varied in ac-
cordance with the rôle concerned and with the
style of play. In some instances the origin of the
species was the determining factor. Those used
in satyr-drama have been already described
(p. 11, and fig. 3). The chorus, as we recall,
regularly impersonated half-human, half-bestial
attendants of Dionysus. But in Old Comedy no
such restriction was imposed. Any group of
creatures, real or fanciful, might be selected by
the poet for representation, and the costumes
were devised in keeping with the choice.
Choruses of bees, ants, frogs, birds, and the like,
reminiscent of the old comus revelries, were
always in favor, as were also those which per-
sonated creatures taken from folktale and myth.

Even inanimate objects, clouds, islands, ships, might be chosen for representation. But most frequently choice was made of one or more types or groups of human beings, such as poets, farmers, charcoal-burners, sorcerers, Athenian women, Thracians, Persians. An instance of a differentiated chorus is found in the *Lysistrata* of Aristophanes: half of the choreutae, twelve in number, represent women; the other half men. The mask, always a prominent feature, was regularly made as amusing as possible with a strong tendency toward exaggerated caricature and the grotesque.

Dress and make-up in the case of the actors also were as ludicrous as a fertile ingenuity could invent. The costume of female characters resembled that worn by women in ordinary life. Male characters wore a short tunic with mantle, if desired, and underneath a garment that somewhat resembled a union-suit, dyed a flesh color and stuffed with pads and bolsters into most unnatural shapes (fig. 19). A regular feature also was a phallus, reminiscent of the Dorian farce which as we have seen (p. 8) appears to have been one of the sources of Attic comedy. Another survival from the primitive mummeries was the mask. This might represent a real person, an individual who like Socrates, Agathon or Euripides was familiar to every Athenian, or it might be purely fictitious. That it was in most instances comically grotesque is made abundantly clear by references in various plays as well as by vase-paintings and statuettes, many of which have been preserved (fig. 19). The shoes worn by the actors were of several different varieties.

Similar to the costumes of old comedy were those worn by the *phlyakes* of Southern Italy (p. 7, fig. 2) and probably in other Greek types of the mime as well.

New Comedy, the comedy of manners, adopted the costumes of ordinary life, except that beneath the tunic was often worn the long-sleeved under-garment familiar to us in comedy of the fifth century (fig. 4). Like much else in this style of drama the details of costume, such as the colors of the garments and the various objects carried or worn by the characters of different types, wallets, staves, oil-flasks and the like, were reduced to a conventional system. Moreover all actors wore the same style of shoe, a sort of soft slipper, which the Greeks called *embas* (ἐμβάs) and the Romans *soccus*, and which became so intimately associated with comic drama that the Latin term early came to signify comedy itself, and in this sense passed into English, as in Milton's familiar lines:

> Then to the well-trod stage anon,
> If Jonson's learned sock be on.[99]

In spite of the great changes that had been wrought in the texture and style of comedy since the days of Aristophanes, so strong was the force of custom that masks continued to be worn, and that too masks of a most distorted and grotesque character (fig. 4). No doubt the vast size of most of the theatres had much to do with the continuance of this practice, but why grotesqueness should have persisted in this period and in this style of drama is difficult to say. For many of the stock characters, such as the irate father, the benevolent old man, the cook, the pimp, the rustic, the heiress, the courtesan, the bully, the swashbuckler, the cunning slave, the miser, the effeminate lover, the parasite, the procuress, there was a mask of particular type. The antiquarian Pollux gives a list of not less than forty-four.[100]

The introduction of New Comedy to Roman audiences took place only fifty years after the death of Menander (291 B.C.) and during the next hundred years occurred the *floruit* of Plautus (died 184 B.C.). What could be more natural then than that the *fabula palliata* (p. 20), which except for the Latin translation and the addition of a few touches of local color was thoroughly Greek, should retain the style of costuming employed in the theatre at Athens? This it did with one important omission: masks were not worn at first nor apparently for more than one hundred years after the epoch-making performances of Livius Andronicus (240 B.C.). Why this was so has never been satisfactorily explained. But they are said to have been made popular by the great actor Roscius and perhaps were introduced shortly before his time by the theatrical managers Cincius Faliscus and Minucius Prothymus.[101]

In the *fabula togata* (p. 20) which rose to popularity for a season after the death of Terence (159 B.C.) a Roman or Italian garb was substituted for the Greek, as also in the *fabula praetexta* or distinctively Roman type of tragedy (p. 19).

Even as the styles of make-up characteristic of satyr-drama and Old Comedy were inherited from earlier mummeries and revelries, so in the case of Greek tragedy the actor's costume was taken over in the main from the cult-ritual of Dionysus. Not all actors of course wore the same style of garb, but that which was distinctive of tragedy comprised a mask, *cothorni* or buskins [102] (they are shown in fig. 3; the two actors in the upper row), and garments consisting of a long, gaily colored, ornamented and sleeved tunic, girt high, and also when desired a mantle or *himation*, which like the tunic might be adorned with elaborate designs (fig. 20). The invention of this costume was ascribed by some ancient writers to Aeschylus, but that this view is unlikely is proved by a pre-Aeschylean black-figured vase, uninfluenced by drama, showing Dionysus and his *thiasos*. The god is represented as wearing a costume so similar to that in use later in tragic drama that the relationship between the two can hardly be doubted.[103] This costume once adopted continued in vogue though with various modifications for hundreds of years, indeed throughout the history of ancient tragedy.

The modifications chiefly to be noted were those introduced to enhance the height and figure of the actor. How early this tendency began is not known, but certainly by the Hellenistic period it was well under way and in

Roman times was carried to excess. One device was to increase the thickness of the sole of the buskins, a device sometimes attributed to Aeschylus, but for which there is no trustworthy evidence in the fifth century. In the Roman period the sole was sometimes of extraordinary thickness (figs. 21 and 22). Another means employed to increase the height of the actor was the prolongation of the upper part of the mask above the forehead, a protuberance known as an *onkos* (figs. 21 and 22). This also apparently was a development of the later periods, though one must admit that the evidence for the fifth century is scant. But the masks shown in the Piraeus relief (fig. 23), as also those depicted on the satyr-vase (fig. 3), both of which date from about 400 B.C., do not have this feature. With the introduction of these two devices, each of which served to enhance the stature of the actor, it became customary also to pad the figure as shown in figure 22, which admirably illustrates the appearance of a Greek tragic actor of the Roman imperial period. The satirist Lucian, who lived in the second century after Christ, describes the tragic actor of his day: " In forming our estimate of tragedy," he says, " let us first consider its externals — the hideous appalling spectacle that the actor presents. His high boots raise him out of all proportion, his head is hidden under an enormous mask; his huge mouth gapes upon the audience as if he would swallow them; to say nothing of the chest-pads and stomach-pads with which he contrives to give himself an artificial corpulence lest his deficiency in this respect should emphasize his disproportionate height:" [104] It is safe to say that Aeschylus and Sophocles would have exclaimed in horror and derision at such a monstrosity. Lucian's tragic actor, as also that of the Rieti statuette (fig. 22), belong to that tasteless age which saw in exaggeration a suitable expression of the imposing and the superhuman, as in the case of the Farnese Heracles of Glycon.

Failure to distinguish clearly between the different periods of ancient drama, to sort with care the various bits of evidence pertaining to each successive stratum, has given rise to many a misconception. Of these none is more glaringly inexcusable than the assumption that Lucian's description and the Rieti statuette faithfully represent the conditions that obtained in the golden age of Pericles. We are told that in tragedy the actor was " a sort of speaking statue, or at least one who in motion, voice and gesture resembled Aristotle's magnanimous man, whose gait is slow and his voice monotonous and deep "; that " these strangely equipped large figures with their immovable faces, which seemed petrified with suffering, and in their gorgeous splendor, advancing slowly with solemn measured movements . . . must have appeared almost like living images of the gods, and when the people heard the beautiful, grave words emanating from these walking statues, they were seized with artistic as well as religious enthusiasm "; that " the dramatist flung his creation against the stage with the greatness of some group in marble; — the crowd hung hushed upon the sufferings of an idealized life, charged with the magnificent hugeness of ethical crises, far removed from common experience." [105]

But the fact is that though much has been written, often from an unleashed imagination, about the style of acting in the fifth century, little is known. A powerful voice, a clear enunciation, a fine ear for rhythm, training in the arts of singing and gesticulation, were no doubt essential to success. But more than these was expected. The plays of the fifth century abound in situations that demand an emotional expres sion, and emotional acting, we may believe, had a large place in the theatre of that time. Moreover the plays of that period, tragedies as well as comedies, contain innumerable passages that call for violent action. The assumption therefore that Greek tragic acting in the days of Aeschylus and Sophocles was " statuesque," far removed from " the realistic portrayal of ordinary human passions," [106] is open to serious question. It implies that Greek tragedy was almost wholly formal and cold, whereas in reality it pulsated with life and was frequently even passionate. Statuesque the acting no doubt was at times, but in general probably little more so than, let us say, when Burbage trod the stage.

FIGURE 21. SCENE FROM A TRAGEDY, ROMAN
PERIOD

From the relief on the grave monument, in Rome, of P. Numitorius
Hilarus. Date about 25 B.C.

XI. INFLUENCES: THE THEATRE; SCENIC ARRANGEMENTS

THE influence of the ancient theatre upon that of modern times is a fascinating subject, but the inquiry involves one in many difficulties.[107] The break, centuries long, with the dramatic traditions of antiquity; the rise of mediaeval drama, unlike the classical in content, form, and manner of presentation; the meagreness of records; the reciprocal influences of public playhouses on the one hand, on the other of performances in universities, schools, and at court — these are some of the conditions which obscure the exact relationship between the two, and that even at the very beginning of the modern age.

Yet that there was a relationship, that the theatre and theatrical traditions of antiquity had a part, even a considerable part, in determining the characteristics of the modern playhouse and even the technique of modern stagecraft, cannot be gainsaid. Whatever may have been the connection of the mime and Atellan

play with certain forms of popular entertainment during the middle ages — a dark and controversial subject — classical legitimate drama
and treatises by ancient writers upon the theatrical usages of antiquity began to make themselves felt during the Renaissance in Italy. This
was due in the first instance and for a long
period to the labors of scholars. Plautus and
Terence in comedy, Seneca in tragedy, Vitruvius in architecture, and Aristotle in literary
criticism were the authors of greatest influence.
To these one may add the Greek tragedians,
Pollux, Horace, Pliny, and even Cassiodorus.

Beginning about the middle of the fifteenth
century under the leadership of Pomponius
Laetus (1425–1498), professor in the University of Rome and founder of the so-called Roman Academy, both ancient plays and new
plays constructed more or less on classical lines
were presented with increasing frequency; and
not at Rome only, but also at Ferrara, Mantua,
Venice, Siena, Naples and other centres of
Italian culture. Nor yet only in Italy; during
the course of the next century the vogue of these
classical and neo-classical plays extended itself
to other European countries as well. In England
the records begin about 1520.

The desire to present classical drama in a manner approximating that of antiquity led naturally to the study of the ancient theatre and ancient methods of representation. Here Vitruvius, Pollux and the comments of scholiasts were the chief sources of information. Preeminent among these was Vitruvius. For the most complete ancient description, preserved to modern times, of the classical type of theatres is found in his authoritative work on architecture, the *De Architectura*. It is supplemented by an explanation of the nature and use of the *periacti* (see p. 110) and a description of the three types of scenes familiar in the Hellenistic and Roman periods: the tragic scene " delineated with columns, pediments, statues, and other objects suited to kings "; the comic scene exhibiting " private dwellings, with balconies and views representing rows of windows, after the manner of ordinary dwellings "; and the satyric scene " decorated with trees, caverns, mountains, and other rustic objects delineated in landscape style." [108] In another part of his treatise, as we have already observed (p. 76), he mentioned the painting of a scene by Agatharcus and the resulting study by Democritus and Anaxagoras of the principles of perspective.

During the classical revival in Italy these brief paragraphs came to exercise an influence far beyond the wildest hopes of their author.

Although some seventy years elapsed from the time of the discovery (1414) of a manuscript of Vitruvius until the publication of the first edition (1486?), his work had already begun to be eagerly studied, and after the appearance of the *editio princeps* edition followed edition, and commentary commentary, not in Italy alone but in all the countries of western Europe. Everywhere the effect was the same. Throughout the period of the Renaissance the word of Vitruvius, as interpreted by the scholars of the day, was law in the field of architecture and was of high authority in the allied arts including that of scenic representation.

But from the start the exigencies of environment led to the adoption of certain modifications of the rules laid down by the great master. On the one hand were the influences exerted by the staging of the mediaeval liturgical drama with its elaborate multiple set and ingenious mechanical devices, and by the inordinate fondness for spectacle as exhibited for example in the case of the *intermezzi* or interludes on the Italian stage; [109] on the other the fact that the

classical dramas were at first regularly pre
sented in " theatres " erected in rectangula
banquet-halls or ball-rooms of princely court!
or in schools and universities.

The effect of the latter condition is clearl;
shown in the earliest illustrated edition of th
De Architectura, that of *Jocundus* (Fra Gio
condo) first published in 1511 and frequentl;
reprinted. His designs for both the Greek and
the Roman theatres call for a rectangular struc
ture. Rectangular too is the plan prepared by
Sebastian Serlio for the second book (1545) of
his *Architettura,* a book that deals with the
theory of perspective particularly as this concerns the art of painting and arranging scenes
on the stage. Rediscovered in the fifteenth century, perspective had become a subject of ab-
sorbing interest long before the publication of
Serlio's important treatise. How he applied it to·
scene decoration is shown by his descriptions
and sketches.

The descriptions which Serlio gives of the
several types of scene were directly inspired by
Vitruvius. " Houses for Tragedies," he writes,
" must be made for great personages, for that
actions of love, strange adventures, and cruell
murthers (as you reade in ancient and modern

tragedies) happen always in the houses of
great Lords, Dukes, Princes, and Kings. Therefore in such cases you must make none but
stately houses." There must be " great Palaces,
large Temples, and divers Houses, both neere
and farre off; broad places filled with Houses,
long streets crost with other wayes; triumphant
Arches, high Pillars or Colummes, Pyramides,
Obeliscens, and a thousand fayre things and
buildings, adorned with innumerable lights."
In " Comicall " scenes " the Houses must be
made as if they were for common or ordinarie
people . . . but specially there must not want
a brawthell or bawdy house, and a great Inn,
and a Church; such things of necessity to be
therein." " The Satiricall Scenes are to represent Satirs, wherein you must place all those
things that be rude and rusticall . . . with
Trees, Rootes, Herbs, Hils and Flowers, and
with some country houses." [110]

The houses employed in these scenes, he di-
rects, should be built on wooden frames covered
with canvas and, with the exception of those in
the rear, should have a front and one side. To
enhance the effect of perspective that portion of
the stage on which the houses were to be constructed should be made to rise gradually from

front to rear and the successive rows of houses carefully foreshortened.

The treatise of Serlio " is of supreme impor- tance to the student of the stage because of its detailed and naïve descriptions. It was impor- tant in the history of the stage because it first formulated the practices of the best craftsmen of its time. . . . There is a distinct indication throughout Serlio's work that the rules of Vitru- vius are becoming rationalized and that they find their justification in their conformity to the demands of verisimilitude." [111]

The next step was taken by the distinguished architect Andrea Palladio, who was commis- sioned by the Olympic Academy of Vicenza to construct a permanent public theatre. Like all the other architects of the day Palladio was an assiduous student of Vitruvius, and the influ- ence of the master was mirrored in almost every feature of the building which Palladio designed. At the rear of the stage was erected a lofty *scaenae frons* elaborately adorned after the Ro- man manner (fig. 24) with a larged arched door- way in the centre flanked by two smaller doors, while two additional entrances at the ends of the stage in the projecting side wings made five in all even as Vitruvius had stipulated.[112] In the construction of the auditorium, however, Palladio introduced a modification of the Vitruvian plans, an innovation that has persisted even to our own day. He arranged the seats in the form of a semi-ellipse instead of a semi-circle, thereby affording a larger proportion of the spectators a good view of the stage.

Begun in the year 1580 this theatre of Palladio was brought to completion by his son in 1584. In the following year, however, on the occasion of a visit to Vicenza of the Empress Maria of Austria, the architect Scamozzi added back of the Palladian *scaenae frons* a permanent scene in perspective with houses and sloping streets (the central one leading to a triumphal archway) after the manner described by Serlio. "The decoration of the scene in perspective painting described by Vitruvius had become a painting in perspective of the separate architectural units of the scene and these in turn were now introduced into the permanent scene wall as perspective or scenic streetways." [113]

This *Teatro Olimpico* of Palladio and Scamozzi is still preserved and is occasionally used for dramatic entertainments. The oldest existing theatre building of modern times in Europe, it is a monument of surpassing interest to all lovers of the drama, not only because it represents in a sense the culmination of the classical period in theatre architecture in Italy, but also because of the immense influence which it exerted upon the development of the playhouse during the seventeenth century.

In Italy this influence was manifested, to cite only one example, in the theatre erected at Parma[114] by Giovanni Battista Aleotti, the so-called *Teatro Farnese*, begun in 1618 but not opened for performances until 1628. In England it profoundly affected the designs created by the distinguished architect and scenic artificer Inigo Jones, Surveyor of His Majesty's Works at the courts of James I and Charles I (1615–43).

Starting with the plans executed by Palladio and Scamozzi, Aleotti introduced several important modifications. The outer stage he made shallower; the inner deeper; while the imposing, but relatively narrow, central door seen in the Palladian theatre he converted into a large triumphal arch occupying in width fully one-half of the *scaenae frons*. Simple as they were these changes were of cardinal significance. They marked the wane of classical influence and the opening of the modern period in the history of the Italian stage.

In England, however, Aleotti had a rival in the person of Inigo Jones who also was keenly interested in the *Teatro Olimpico*, of which he wrote a detailed description under date of "Sundaie ye 23 of September 1613." Designs for a theatre project have recently been discovered and published by Mr. William Grant Keith,[115] which startlingly resemble on the one hand the plan of the *Teatro Olimpico*, on the other the stage arrangements of the *Teatro Farnese*. Yet they probably antedated the theatre at Parma by several years.

As a scenic artificer Jones was employed chiefly to arrange the settings for the elaborate masques presented at the courts of James I and Charles I, and for a time worked in collaboration with Ben Jonson, not to mention others, and toward the end of his career with William Davenant, who long entertained the plan of erecting a public opera-house and of presenting operatic performances in the elaborate spectacular manner familiar at the time in Italy. This plan at last came to fruition. In 1656 Davenant presented at the Rutland House the first opera seen in England, *The Siege of Rhodes*, the designs for which, as Davenant himself tells us,[116] were executed by John Webb, who was a nephew of Inigo Jones, had for many years been his assistant, and had inherited his plans and possessions. In 1658-9 Davenant produced operas at the Cockpit in Drury Lane, and later moved to a playhouse he had fitted up in Lincoln's Inn Fields, and known as the Duke's Theatre or Duke's House. Thus the traditions established by Jones in connection with the masques at court were transmitted directly to the post-Restoration period and the picture-frame stage.

Many drawings by Jones, both ground plans and elevations, have been preserved and are familiar to all students of the stage. There have been preserved also descriptions by Jones himself or by others of the settings he devised and the various mechanical appliances he employed. These are of fascinating interest on many accounts, but two features only need be mentioned here: his use of the proscenium arch and his experiments with different types of movable scenery.

Exactly when and where the proscenium arch was introduced are matters for conjecture. As we have seen, the stage of Aleotti's theatre at Parma had a great triumphal archway, as did also Jones' design for a theatre-project of presumably somewhat earlier date. But that an arch was employed prior to these in the staging of masques at the court of James I is clear from certain passages in the writings of Jonson and of Jones. An anticipation of the arch structure was employed in the staging of Jonson's *Masque of Hymen* (1606), two huge statues of Hercules and Atlas supporting the firmament. In 1608 for Jonson's *Hue and Cry after Cupid* the scene was flanked by " two pilasters, charged with spoils and trophies of Love and his mother . . . and overhead two personages, Triumph and Victory, in flying postures, and twice so big as the life, in place of the arch, and holding a garland of myrtle for the key." [117] In 1610 there was an arch for Daniel's *Tethys Festival* and from this time on the use of an arch or rectangular frame was habitual.

As has just been stated the origin of these types of proscenia is in doubt. Probably a classical origin should not be claimed for them, but they are pertinent to this discussion if only for the reason that with their introduction there entered also the use of movable scenery, in connection with which the influence of the ancients is clearly discovered.

The experiments of Inigo Jones with movable

scenes began apparently in the summer of 1605 on the occasion of the presentation of a Latin tragedy at Christ Church, Oxford, and shortly after his return from Italy. To effect the changing of scenes in this play Jones made use of *periacti* as described by Vitruvius (p. 110). The scene "was adorned with stately pillars, which pillars would turn about, by reason whereof, with the help of other painted cloths, their stage did vary three times in the acting of one tragedy." [118] This innovation was apparently not regarded as satisfactory and so far as we know the experiment was not repeated, but it is an interesting example of a modern attempt to rehabilitate an ancient device.

Jones also experimented with a *machina versatilis*, a counterpart in a sense of the ancient *scaena versilis* (p. 109). Thus for Jonson's *Masque of Hymen* (1606) the "machine of the spectacle" was a great globe which turned to reveal the masques; for the *Masque of Queens* (1609) there was "a glorious and magnificent building, figuring the House of Fame, in the top of which were discovered the twelve Masquers, sitting upon a throne triumphal . . . the throne wherein they sat, being *machina versatilis*,

suddenly changed; and in the place of it appeared Fama Bona." [119]

But it was the *scaena ductilis* upon which
Jones finally settled as the most satisfactory
method of shifting scenes. His experiments extended over several years and at last, apparently
in 1636, culminated in the invention of wings
or shutters which could be moved laterally in
grooves. These were employed perhaps for the
first time in plays presented at Christ Church,
Oxford, and are described by Anthony à Wood
in his account of the royal visit to Oxford on that
occasion. [120] The first play, *Passions Calmed,*
by Strode, " was acted on a goodly stage . . .
(which) had on it three or four openings on each
side thereof, and partitions between them, much
resembling the desks or studies in a library, out
of which the Actors issued forth. The said partitions they could draw in and out at their pleasure upon a sudden, and thrust out new in their
places according to the nature of the screen,
whereon were represented Churches, Dwelling-
houses, Palaces, etc., which for its variety bred
very great admiration." How these shutters
were arranged is well shown in the design by
Jones for Davenant's masque *Salmacida Spolia,*
presented in 1640, and a similar plan by Webb

for Davenant's opera *The Siege of Rhodes*
(1656) has recently been published by Mr.
Keith.[121] From the court and academic theatres
this device, based in the first instance upon the
scaena ductilis of the ancients, passed over to
the public stage, where it remained in vogue as
the accepted method of shifting scenes until the
invention of the " box-set " about the middle of
the last century.

The English stage of the seventeenth century
was not alone in its use of movable scenery.
Mechanical devices for changing scenes were
known also in Italy and presumably elsewhere
as well. But, writes Professor Thorndike, " the
various steps by which the moving scenes were
improved by Inigo Jones seem due to his invention . . . the question is not of transformations
and machines, but of a change of scene by
movable flat frames. In this particular I know
of no contemporary advance on the English
court masques." [122]

Of the use of machines upon the Renaissance
stage there is little need to speak, as mechanical
contrivances of bewildering variety had long
been employed and classical influence is uncertain. But the *deus ex machina* played a prominent part in the dramatic criticism of the time,

and was so frequently resorted to that the word *machina* came to mean " the skies or coūterfit heauen over the stage, from whence some god appeared or spoke.[123]

But one device employed in the sixteenth and the early part of the seventeenth centuries deserves particular mention. This was a front-curtain which was lowered at the beginning of a play and raised at the close after the manner of the Roman *aulaeum* (p. 108). The earliest clue to its employment on the modern stage, according to Mr. Lawrence,[124] " is afforded in the *Orlando Furioso* of Ariosto, the first forty cantos of which were published in 1515 ":

> As *when at fall of curtain we espy*
> M*id thousand brilliant lamps the scenery fair,*
> T*riumphal arches, towers that fret the sky,*
> S*tatues, the gleam of gold and pictures rare.*[125]

One suspects that Pomponius Laetus was responsible for its introduction. However that may be, records prove that its use was common in Italy throughout the sixteenth century and even later. From Italy it passed to France and England, into the latter of which countries it was introduced presumably by Inigo Jones. At any rate the earliest trace of it in England is

FIGURE 22. TRAGIC ACTOR OF THE ROMAN
IMPERIAL PERIOD

This is the so-called Rieti statuette in Naples. The rectangular supports beneath the feet fitted into the
base and were not intended to be seen

said to be found in Ben Jonson's *Masque of Blackness* (1605), which Jonson himself described. " First, for the scene (i.e. front curtain) was drawn a *landtschap* [landscape] consisting of small woods, and here and there a void place filled with huntings; which falling, an artificial sea was seen to shoot forth," etc.[126] The stage arrangements for this play were executed by Jones. That the aulaeum continued in use for several years after this is clear from the account given by Orazio Busino, chaplain to the Venetian Ambassador, of the presentation of Jonson's *Pleasure Reconciled to Virtue* in 1618: " In an instant a large curtain dropped," etc.[127] Ultimately, however, apparently about 1631, this rather clumsy device borrowed from the ancients was superseded by the modern top-roller curtain. With its disappearance classical influence upon the mechanical aspects of the Renaissance stage may be said to have come to an end.[128]

XII.   INFLUENCES: THE DRAMA

THE drama of Greece developed to the full bloom of maturity in the city of Athens in the fifth century before Christ, and by a process as natural as the flowering of a rose. The product of social, religious and artistic impulses, it was an expression of the life of the people — the whole people — at a time of greatly intensified vitality. With the waning of this vitality the period of decadence began. Thereupon the drama either changed its form, as in the case of comedy, or sank to mediocrity as in that of tragedy, and became gradually artificial, insipid, a pale reflection of the glories of the golden age. Just as ancient exuberant, lyrical comedy died with Aristophanes, so in a sense the style of tragedy which is most typically Hellenic came to an end with the death of Sophocles.

New Comedy which arose to supplant the old was so simple in its form, so deft in the construction of its plots, so universal in its appeal, that it was readily transplanted and propa-

gated elsewhere than in Greece, and flourished
not only in all parts of the ancient Roman
Empire, but in Renaissance Europe as well.
Through adaptations and imitations of Plautus
and Terence it wielded a formative influence
upon the development of modern comedy. We
come upon a hint of this already in the tenth
century in the little plays by the famous Hrotsvitha, the nun of Gandersheim. But what
effect, if any, these and possibly other similar
productions had upon the history of the drama
during the succeeding centuries is not known.
For us the effective influence of classical comedy begins in the fifteenth century; representa-
tions of the plays of Plautus and Terence, both
in Latin and in translation; adaptations and
original compositions in endless succession
based on Plautine and Terentian models. The
stream of influence which took its rise chiefly
at Rome under Pomponius Laetus (p. 150) and
at Ferrara under Duke Ercole I, the Maecenas
of Renaissance drama, swept on as a mighty
torrent through the dramatic literature for
hundreds of years.

Comedy by becoming thoroughly denation-
alized was enabled to survive the downfall of
Hellenic civilization and became a heritage of

the modern world. Quite different was the fate of Greek tragedy. Even in ancient Rome it was an exotic; in Renaissance Europe it was choked and overshadowed by the ranker growth of Senecan tragedy. The florid, rhetorical, declamatory, debased dramas of the Neronian era, with their horrors and ghosts, their interminable speeches, their frigid intermezzic choruses — these it was that suited the tastes of the age, elicited the praise of scholars, and were taken as the models for neo-classical tragedy. From the time of Mussato's *Ecerinis* (about 1314) for three hundred years the sinister figure of Seneca dominated the tragic stage; whereas Sophocles and Euripides, though some of their plays were occasionally performed and even imitated, were unable to stem the Senecan tide and have exercised but a minimum influence upon the modern drama.

To example precept was added. From Aristotle's *Poetics* and the *Ars Poetica* of Horace, taken in conjunction with the plays themselves, rules for dramatic construction were deduced and erected into a rigid system of determining principles. Every play should have five acts. Were not Seneca's tragedies so divided, and did not Horace so prescribe? There should be unity

FIGURE 23. GREEK TRAGIC ACTORS

From a relief found at the Piraeus, now in Athens. Date about 400 B.C. To the right Dionysus reclining on a couch with a young woman sitting at his feet. To the left three tragic actors. Two of the actors are holding *tympana* or tambourines

of time. Did not Aristotle (*Poetics*, V) remark that " tragedy endeavors, so far as possible, to confine itself to a single revolution of the sun, or but slightly to exceed the limit "? There should be unity of place. Did not Maggi anticipate and Castelvetro definitely formulate this law? Little matter that the Greek playwright did not regard unity of time and unity of place as coercive principles of dramatic technique, that he observed them rather merely as natural and prevailing, though violable, traditions of his art. Little matter that had the Italian scholars of the sixteenth century, Cintio and Robortello, Castelvetro and Scaliger, and a host of others, been more observant of the facts, the bastard " unities " might never have been erected into a dogma of dramatic art. They were so erected, and this must therefore count as one of the influences of ancient drama upon the modern, a baleful influence it may be, based at least in part upon error and misconception, but none the less cogent and binding.

A long period of gestation preceded the birth of humanistic drama, and from time to time there were certain premonitory signs which heralded the coming event, such as the little plays of Hrotsvitha, already mentioned, in-

spired by the comedies of Terence, and in
the twelfth century the dramatic poems of the
French humanists Vital de Blois and Matthieu
de Vendôme, the *Geta* of the former, of the
latter the *Miles Gloriosus,* both revealing the
influence of Plautus. But it was not until
the early years of the fourteenth century that
modern dramatic literature was born.

The beginning of modern drama may be
dated from the year, perhaps about 1314, when
Alberto Mussato, a native of Padua and a contemporary of Dante, produced his first tragedy,
the *Ecerinis.* This brief play (there are only
629 verses), though it deals with a modern subject, the misdeeds and death of the detested
Ecelino, tyrant of Padua, is almost entirely
Senecan in form. The language is Latin, the
speeches are iambic senarii, the play is divided
into five portions each closing with a choral ode
(one of which like a part of the third ode in the
Medea of Seneca absurdly consists of Sapphic
stanzas), the action is narrated rather than
presented to the eye, sententious utterances
abound. At the best it is a dull performance, as
is also its companion-piece the *Achilleis,* which
treats of a time-worn theme; but even so these
two plays, because they stand at the very

threshold of the modern era, merit our attention. A few years later, sometime before 1331, Petrarch, ardent admirer of Plautus and Terence, wrote a Latin comedy, *Philologia*, about which, however, unfortunately almost nothing is known. Boccaccio praises it and speaks of its Terentian reminiscences.[129]

After these and a few other early pieces now mostly shrouded in the mists of uncertainty there were still many years of waiting. It is as though neo-classical drama had been born before its time and incubation must supplement gestation. Indeed it was not until the fifteenth century that lusty growth commenced; not till the sixteenth and seventeenth centuries that maturity was attained.

But to trace in detail the history of modern drama as influenced by classical models is not our purpose. The story has been often repeated. Let it suffice to note merely some of the features of technique which the ancient drama impressed upon certain species of modern literature.

Some of these may be dismissed at once as instances of what one may term incidental imitation; they are either isolated phenomena such as the occurrence of a *parabasis* in August von Platen's *Die Verhängnissvolle Gabel* (1826),

the *Néphélococugie* (1578) of Pierre le Loyer,
and a few other comedies reminiscent of Aristophanes; or stylistic peculiarities of slight
significance like the occasional use of *stichomy-
thia* or one-line dialogue, by certain Renaissance playwrights in imitation of the ancients.
Matters such as these are but eddies at the edge
of the stream. It is the main current of influence
which we would explore.

Of this influence two effects have been already indicated: the development and application of the doctrine of the unities, based in part
upon the treatises of literary critics, and the
adaptation of the five-act form. The growth of
the doctrine of the unities in the writings of the
Italian critics has been admirably traced by
Professor Spingarn,[130] who points out, what is
now universally recognized, that it is to Italy
and not to France, as Dryden supposed, that the
world owed this doctrine. But it was in France
nevertheless that the doctrine of the unities of
time and place became most firmly established.
From the time of the famous controversy over
Corneille's *Cid* (1636) until, two hundred years
later, they were finally toppled from their
throne by the titanic blows dealt by Victor
Hugo in his *Cromwell* (1827) and *Hernani*

(1830), they held unrelenting sway over the French stage. Among the English the most distinguished playwright to advocate and observe them was Jonson, though he did so with discretion. Shakespeare knew them only to ignore them, except in his *Tempest*. But with the coming of French influence in the Restoration period the " Italian unities " became fixed laws for the English stage and remained in force for more than an hundred years. If they reappear occasionally in dramatic literature since the " Battle of Hernani," as in the *Francillon* of the younger Dumas, the *Ghosts* of Ibsen, the *Idol Breaker* of Charles Rann Kennedy, John Galsworthy's *Joy* and Robert Louis Stevenson's *Beau Austin,* they are due to choice, not to subservience to a tyrannical law. The ancient Greeks, as we have seen (pp. 107, 120), not only on occasion disregarded unity of place but repeatedly accelerated and idealized the time, conventionally reducing hours and days to minutes. In many a Greek drama unity of time was a mere figment of the imagination.

To the " Procrustean framework in five acts," [131] which began to take shape under the hand of Euripides, was completed by the labors of the Alexandrians, commended by Horace and adopted by Seneca, practically all modern play-wrights, with however certain notable excep-tions, felt constrained to fit their dramas, both tragedies and comedies, throughout a period of more than five hundred years, even from the time of Mussato to the new era inaugurated by Dumas *fils* and Ibsen. No influence of the ancient drama upon the modern has been more far-reaching than this, and none so vicious. In menially submitting to the strait-jacket of the supposed requirement pseudo-classicism dis-played the crassest stupidity.

In comparison with this the writing of pro-logues and epilogues was but an innocent diver-sion. The custom which like knee-buckles and powdered wigs once had a tremendous vogue and which like these has long since lost its charm, rested in the main upon a classical tradi-tion. In the main, — for ecclesiastical plays of the Middle Ages sometimes had these features. But there can be little doubt that the detached and semi-detached prologues and epilogues, which one associates more particularly with the name of Dryden but which were popular both before his time as well as afterward, were sug-gested by the examples of Terence and Plautus. Over these we need not linger. The examples are

legion, one of the earliest being that by Angelo
Poliziano written for a performance of the
Menaechmi of Plautus (Florence, 1488), a
fusillade of criticism against Latin comedies in
prose, pedagogical abuses, and hypocrisy in
monkish garb.

Of far greater significance for our purposes
are prologues and epilogues that are integral
parts of the plays to which they belong. These
also are legion and the influence of Seneca, that
is ultimately of Euripides, is constantly in evidence, as in the opening scene of Lodovico
Dolce's *Giocasta* (printed in 1549), a translation of a Latin version of the *Phoenissae* of
Euripides and translated in turn by George
Gascoigne and Francis Kinwelmershe: *Jocasta*
(1566). Other examples are the dialogue at the
beginning of Gian Giorgio Trissino's *Sofonisba*
(1515), the speech of the ghost of Antonius in
Cléopatre Captive (1552) of Étienne Jodelle,
that of the ghost of Andrea in the *Spanish
Tragedy* (1592) by Thomas Kyd, of Rumour in
Shakespeare's *Henry IV,* Part II, and others
without number. Far superior to these is the
speech of Gloster in *Richard III,* an admirable
exposition of both situation and character.

The closing address of Richmond in the last

mentioned play bears a striking resemblance —
it is not imitation — to the speeches of the *dei
ex machina* in Euripides which, as we have
already observed (p. 116), partake of the nature of an epilogue.

Inter their bodies as becomes their births.
Proclaim a pardon to the soldiers fled
That in submission will return to us.

   .   .   .   .   .   .

O, now let Richmond and Elizabeth,
The true succeeders of each royal house,
By God's fair ordinance conjoin together!
And let their heirs (God, if thy will be so!)
Enrich the time to come with smooth-faced peace,
With smiling plenty, and fair prosperous days!

In the nature of an epilogue also are the brief
disquisition of young Arthur at the end of the
anonymous *How a Man May Chuse a Good
Wife from a Bad* (c. 1612), and the long address of Eubulus at the close of *Gorboduc*
(1562). Imitations of the Plautine epilogic tags
also abound. One example will suffice: Shakespeare's *All's Well that Ends Well:*

The king's a beggar, now the play is done;
All is well ended, if this suit be won,

[176]

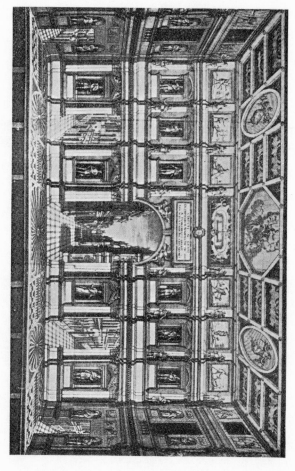

FIGURE 24. THE STAGE AND "PERSPECTIVES" OF THE TEATRO OLIMPICO AT VICENZA

That you express content; which we will pay,
With strife to please you, day exceeding day.
Ours be your patience then, and yours our parts;
Your gentle hands lend us and take our hearts.

In Menander's comedies, as has recently been discovered, the isolated prologue made popular by Euripides was sometimes postponed and became, so to say, an interlogue. An interesting parallel to this is the speech of Interpretour at the close of the first part of Bishop Bale's *Kynge Johan* (*c.* 1548), in which is set forth at length the outline of the succeeding portion. Somewhat similar, though on a grander scale and in a more poetic vein, are the speeches of Chorus in Shakespeare's *Henry V,* which taken together, with the exception of the epilogic verses at the close, constitute a magnificent prologue distributed through the play.

In the *Spanish Tragedy* the ghost of Andrea and the Spirit of Revenge not only open the play, but bring it to a fitting close. They also " serve for chorus in this tragedy " and round out each act with a bit of dialogue. Choruses and other lyrics there had been in ecclesiastical drama and these doubtless were not without influence upon the dramatic literature of the modern age. But it was from the ancients that Renaissance tragedy borrowed the choral interludes. Whether expositional in character or reflective, whether in blank verse or ·rhymed couplets or lyric stanzas, these Renaissance intermezzic choruses were seldom dramatically convincing. The reason is not far to seek. Among the Greeks the chorus was the very root and stem from which the drama grew; among the moderns, a grafted alien shoot or at its worst, merely an artificial flower hung among the branches. Between Aeschylus or Sophocles on the one hand, on the other Seneca, Loschi, Trissino, Dolce, Jodelle, Garnier, Marlowe, Jonson — name whom one will — what a world of difference! In the one case lyric stasima and dramatic episodes interdependent, fitted and bonded together in a flawless harmony; in the other the interstices between the acts filled with an inadherent mortar of speech and song.

Again it was Seneca who pointed the way; again Mussato who blazed the trail. Many were those who traveled the path thus opened, until it became deep-worn with the use of centuries. In recent years, however, only an occasional wayfarer has ventured therealong, one of these the doughty Drinkwater. The beautiful verses

spoken by the two Chroniclers in his *Abraham
Lincoln* serve essentially the same purpose as
the chorus in *Gorboduc* or *Doctor Faustus* or
Henry V or Seneca's *Medea*.

In comparison with Seneca the Greek tragedians have had in modern times an almost
negligible following. For Greek tragedy particularly in its handling of the chorus is more
difficult of imitation. Aside, then, from repro-
ductions both in the original and in translation,
of which there have been many notable examples,[132] the type has appeared only sporadically, except indeed during the Renaissance period when it enjoyed a considerable vogue. But
even at that time, though the form might be
Greek, the tone was too often predominantly
Senecan. The examples are too numerous to
mention. Trissino's *Sofonisba* (1515) may serve
as an illustration. It reflects the influence both
of Sophocles and Euripides. Less successful are
Rosmunda (1516) and *Oreste* (1525, based on
Euripides' *Iphigenia Taurica*) of Giovanni
Rucellai. In general Renaissance Italian trag-
edy was as frigid as the plays of the notorious
Theognis whom Aristophanes ridicules in his
Acharnians. "Applying rules of Aristotle and
Horace, travestying Sophocles and Euripides,

copying the worst faults of Seneca, patching, boggling, rehandling, misconceiving, devising petty traps instead of plots, mistaking blood-shed and brutality for terror, attending to niceties of diction, composing commonplace sentences for superfluous choruses, intent on everything but the main points of passion, character and action, they produce the dreariest *caput mortuum* of unintelligent industry which it is the melancholy duty of historians to chronicle." [133]

More recent attempts to follow Greek tragic form, Milton's *Samson Agonistes,* Racine's *Esther,* Schiller's *Braut von Messina,* Matthew Arnold's *Merope,* Swinburne's *Atalanta in Calydon* and the like, no matter how beautiful as dramatic poems, have rarely been seen upon the public stage. The Greek tragic form flourished only among the Greeks; for the rest of the world it has been, and continues to be, an exotic.

In the realm of comedy it was Plautus and Terence, not Aristophanes, that appealed to the Renaissance playwrights. Modern comedy, therefore, has usually lacked a chorus. But there have been exceptions. One may mention the *Henno* (1497) of the German humanist

Johann Reuchlin, the anonymous *Eckius De-
dolatus* (sixteenth century), replete with quotations from Aristophanes, the *Néphélococugie*
(1578) of Pierre le Loyer, an adaptation of the
Birds with a parabasis as well as chorus, and a
few others. A complete list would be neither
long nor impressive. Even *Les Plaideurs* of
Racine, though inspired by the *Wasps*, is non-
choral in form, as are also his tragic *Iphigenie
en Aulide* and Goethe's *Iphigenie auf Tauris*.
Old Comedy like tragedy of the fifth century
can not claim a numerous progeny.

But opera, both light and serious, bears a
certain resemblance to Greek drama, to which
indeed it is in part indebted. Though complex
in origin the opera as a distinct genre was invented in Italy toward the close of the sixteenth
century and as a direct result of the efforts of
the Florentine Giovanni Bardi and his friends,
Giulio Caccini, Jacopo Peri, Vicenzo Galilei,
Ottavio Rinuccini, and others to discover a style
of singing suitable for dramatic purposes. In
their search they went direct to the drama of the
ancient Greeks, which they believed had been
declaimed in musical tones. " Their experiments
resulted in the invention of a kind of musical
utterance that was half way between speech and

song, a heightening of the inflections of ordinary speech, rising now and then in more impassioned moments into irregular melodious cadences, at times even giving way to a burst of florid passages on a single syllable. Out of intonation came recitative and air. . . . It is not incorrect to say that in the Bardi circle somewhere about 1590 recitative was invented and with it the modern opera was founded." [134]

Thus opera was in part the child of Greek drama. But it soon departed from the simple form given it by Peri and Caccini. Gorgeous spectacle and intricate musical effects with elaborate and bewildering orchestration almost snuffed out the histrionic element. Between the majestic severity of the *Agamemnon* of Aeschylus and the overpowering fury of Wagner's *Götterdämmerung* or the passionate excesses of the *Elektra* of Strauss there is indeed little comparison.

NOTES AND BIBLIOGRAPHY

NOTES

[The abbreviation B. refers to the Bibliography on pp. 193–198.]

1. Milton, *Il Penseroso*, 97 ff.

2. Greek αὐλός, Latin *tibia*, usually translated 'flute.' But it had a deeper and richer tone than a flute, and resembled rather the clarinet or oboe (see fig. 3).

3. By the *Parian Chronicle*, an inscription containing dates of Greek political, religious, and literary history. See F. Jacoby, *Das Marmor Parium*, Berlin, 1904, 13.

4. For a brief bibliography of the origin, composition, etc. of Old Comedy see B. nos. 26 and 96.

5. For Middle and New Comedy see B. no. 51.

6. According to Suidas, Pratinas was " the first to write satyr-plays." He established himself in Athens toward the end of the sixth century B.C.

7. Sileni were equine; satyrs, apparently caprine. Yet the satyrs in Attic satyr-drama appear to have been equine (see fig. 3). A completely satisfactory solution of this perplexing problem has not yet been found. See B. no. 26, pp. 1 (footnote 1), 24 ff.

8. *Poetics*, Chap. IV.

9. The subjects mentioned in this and the last two preceding paragraphs are discussed at length in the larger treatises and in many special articles. See B. no. 26; also nos. 73 and 86.

10. See R. C. Flickinger, " Tragedy and Satyric Drama," in *Classical Philology*, VIII, 269 ff. (1913).

11. Horace, *Ars Poetica*, 276, remarks that Thespis is said to have carried his plays about on wagons. The matter is very obscure; see B. no. 5, pp. 87, 185.

12. See B. no. 36, chap. VI.

13.   On the drama at Rome see B. nos. 20, 23, 31, 51, 52, 53, 74, 79, 80, 82, and 89.

14.   One *fabula praetexta* has been preserved: the *Octavia*, of unknown authorship but traditionally ascribed to Seneca. See F. J. Miller, *The Tragedies of Seneca*, Chicago, 1907, 417 ff.

15.   *Ad Fam.*, VII. 2.

16.   *Epist.*, II. 1. 182.

17.   The toga resembled in shape the segment of a circle; the pallium was rectangular.

18.   Livy, XXXIX. 22; Polybius, XXX. 13.

19.   Suetonius, *Julius*, 39; *Octavianus*, 43.

20.   *Brutus*, 21.

21.   See A. Deissmann, *Light from the Ancient East*, 59 (transl. of L. R. M. Strachan, New York, 1910); also *Bible Studies*, 77 (transl. of R. Grieve, Edinburgh, 1909).

22.   *Epist.*, II. 1. 145 ff.

23.   See W. Smith, *The Commedia dell' Arte*, New York, 1912, and P. L. Duchartre, *La comédie italienne*, Paris, 1924? Each contains an important bibliography. See also B. no. 20.

24.   *Ad. Fam.*, IX. 16.

25.   Livy, VII. 2.

26.   On the language of gesture see especially Quintilian, XI. 3. 85 ff.; also B. nos. 81 and 94.

27.   B. No. 57, I, 238.

28.   B. nos. 12 and 55; also J. S. Tunison, *Dramatic Traditions of the Dark Ages*, Chicago, 1907.

29.   See B. no. 37, Appendix C.

30.   See W. A. Dittmer, *The Fragments of Athenian Comic Didascaliae Found in Rome*, Leiden, 1923, 4n. and 42 f.

31.   *Acharnians*, 9 ff.; *Frogs*, 868.

32.   The statement is preserved in one of the *hypotheseis* prefixed to the *Frogs*.

33.   Our authority is the ancient *Life of Euripides*.

34.   *Or.*, XXI. 152; 178; 180.

35.   For the literature bearing upon the subject of this chapter see B. nos. 27, 28, 31 and 35.

36. Macrobius says (*Sat.*, II. 10) that R. received 1000 denarii (4000 sestertii) for each performance, while Pliny, *N. H.*, VII. 39, states that his annual income from this source was 500,000 sestertii. This would make 125 performances a year. But possibly the figures are not correct.

37. Censorinus, XVII. 8. The Augustan celebration mentioned in the text assumed a *saeculum* of 110 years. For a concise discussion of this subject see J. E. Sandys, *A Companion to Latin Studies*,³ Cambridge, 1921, 111 f.

38. See T. Mommsen, " Commentarium ludorum saecularium quintorum," in *Mon. Antichi dei Lincei*, I. 619 ff. (1892); also in *Ephemeris Epigraphica*, VIII. 222 ff. (1892); M. S. Slaughter, " The Acta ludorum saec. quint. and the Carm. Saec. of Horace," in *Trans. Amer. Phil. Assoc.*, XXVI. 69 ff. (1895); also J. Frei, *De certaminibus thymelicis*, Basel, 1900.

39. Line 157 of the inscription describing the Ludi Saeculares; see the preceding note.

40. See Reisch, art. " Ludi astici," in Pauly-Wissowa.

41. Tacitus, *Ann.*, I. 77; IV. 14; XIII. 28; Suetonius, *Tiberius*, 37.

42. Terence, *Hecyra*, Prolog. II.

43. Shakespeare, *Hamlet*, III. 2.

44. Did the *proskenion* originate in Athens or in the Peloponnesus or in Southern Italy or in Asia Minor? Was it intended to serve as a background, or as a stage? If at first as a background, when and where did it become a stage? These questions have not yet been answered to the satisfaction of all. See B. nos. 2, 22 and 26. For the *logeion* see B. no. 26, p. 59. Another troublesome term is *theologeion* (speaking place for divinities), which occurs only in Pollux *Onomasticon*, IV. 127 and 130. What it was is not known; see B. no. 26, p. 60.

45. The purpose of these ramps is not known and has given rise to much speculation. See B. no. 37, p. 125, and B. no. 68.

46. On the *thyromata* see K. F. W. Dittenberger, *Sylloge Inscriptionum Graecarum*,² II. 587, note 56. 1900.

47. Thucydides, II, 41.

48. Milton, *Par. Reg.*, IV, 240.

49. *Poetics*, Chap. IV.

50. VII, *Praefatio* 11, transl. of Morgan; see B. no. 92.

51. J. Six, "Agatharchus," in *Journal of Hellenic Studies*, XL. 180 ff., esp. 189 (1920).

52. Alcamenes was an Athenian sculptor of the latter half of the fifth century B.C.

53. See J. G. Frazer, *Pausanias*, II. 219 ff.

54. B. no. 26, pp. 88 ff.; no. 66, pp. 53 ff.; also nos. 9 and 95.

55. See my "Problems of the Proskenion," in *University of California Publications in Classical Philology*, VII. no. 5 (1923).

56. The height and depth of the Neronian stage are unknown. Dörpfeld has even advanced the theory — improbable in my judgment — that there was no stage at this period.

57. At least one of these appears to have been erected before Hadrian became Emperor; see J. R. Wheeler, "The Theatre of Dionysus," in *Papers Amer. School at Athens*, I. 149 ff. (1885).

58. For a reproduction and discussion of this frieze see especially A. B. Cook, *Zeus*, Cambridge, 1914, vol. I. 708 ff. and plate XL. It is erroneous to suppose, as some have done, that the heads of the figures were removed at the time of the construction of the Phaedrian stage. The evidence is all to the contrary.

59. VIII. 93.

60. For the theatre at Corinth see T. L. Shear, "Excavations at Corinth in 1925," in *American Journal of Archaeology*, XXIX. 381 ff. (1925); and "Excavations at Corinth in 1926," in *Ibid.*, XXX. 444 ff. (1926).

61. Livy, XL. 51.

62. Gellius, X. 1. 6–10.

63. Valerius Maximus, II. 4. 2; Livy, *Epitome*, 48; Augustine, *De Civ. Dei*, I. 31; Tacitus, *Ann.*, XIV. 21.

64. Livy, XXXIV. 44.

65. Pliny, *N. H.*, XXXIV. 36; XXXVI. 114; etc.

66. *Pompey*, 42.

NOTES

67. Pliny, *N. H.*, VIII. 65, gives the date as 11 B.C.

68. Transl. of A. S. Way (*Loeb Classical Library*).

69. From a poem by Austin Dobson, "When Burbage Played," in *Poetical Works*, Oxford, 1923, 331.

70. See B. no. 25.

71. Vitruvius, VII. 5. 5, transl. of M. H. Morgan.

72. See W. J. Woodhouse, "The Scenic Arrangements of the Philoctetes of Sophocles," in *Journal of Hellenic Studies*, XXXII. 239 ff. (1912).

73. For the evidence see B. no. 70.

74. Shakespeare, *M. N. D.*, V. 1. 18.

75. *Pro Caelio*, 27.

76. *Epist.*, II. 1. 189 ff., transl. of E. C. Wickham, Oxford, 1903.

77. *Georgics*, III. 24 ff., transl. of A. S. Way, London, 1912.

78. V. 6. 8, transl. of Morgan.

79. See J. A. Cramer, *Anecdota Graeca Par.*, Oxford, 1839–41, I. 19.

80. A bibliography will be found in B. no. 2, Chap. VI; see also next note.

81. See B. no. 26, pp. 284 ff.

82. See B. no. 90, Appendix I.

83. For the evidence see B. no. 71.

84. *Onomasticon*, IV. 121 ff.

85. Pollux, *Onom.*, IV. 128.

86. See B. no. 26, pp. 296 ff.

87. On this subject see B. no. 15, and B. no. 59, Chap. III.

88. Verses 290–305.

89. See T. Frank, "Horace on Contemporary Poetry," in *The Classical Journal*, XIII. 550 ff., esp. p. 561 (1918); see also B. no. 55.

90. *Ars Poetica*, 189 ff., transl. of Sir Theodore Martin, Edinburgh, 1898.

91. See B. no. 10.

92. But see W. Ridgeway, "Euripides in Macedon," in *Class. Quarterly*, XX. 1 ff. (1926).

93. In the ancient *Life of Aeschylus*.

NOTES

94. The two quotations are from Lucas (B. no. 55), pp. 20 and 24.

95. B. no. 37, p. 229.

96. For the evidence upon which this and the next two paragraphs are based see B. Warnecke, art. " Histrio," in Pauly-Wissowa.

97. As by Rees (B. no. 69).

98. *De falsa legatione,* 10.

99. *L'Allegro,* 131 ff.

100. *Onomasticon,* IV. 143 ff. As is well known Mr. Gordon Craig has for many years been earnestly advocating the use of masks on the modern stage, so far without noteworthy success. For one instance of their use, see A. Forman, " The Mask in the Theatre, the Revival of an Old Art," in *Drama,* XII. 113 (1922). For the construction of masks see R. I. Gears, " Masks of Classic and Modern Times," in *Scientific American,* XCV. 248 ff., 260 ff. (1906).

101. See note 96 (above) and B. nos. 77 and 78.

102. See B. no. 83. The *cothornos* (Latin *cothurnus*) was a loosely fitting boot reaching to the calf and worn especially by women. The effeminate Dionysus was supposed to wear cothorni, hence their use in the theatre.

103. See B. no. 5, fig. 96.

104. *De Saltatione.* 27 (transl. of H. W. and F. G. Fowler, Oxford, 1905).

105. The quotations are respectively, from Campbell (B. no. 7), p. 88; Mantzius (B. no. 57), I. 187; L. M. Watt, *Attic and Elizabethan Tragedy,* London, 1908, p. 27.

106. B. no. 37, p. 277.

107. In the preparation of this chapter I have been indebted chiefly to B. no. 8; also to nos. 1, 14, 44, 45, 50, 61, 88 and 90.

108. V. 6. 9, transl. of Morgan.

109. See J. Burckhardt, *The Civilization of the Renaissance in Italy,* transl. of S. G. C. Middlemore, London, 1898.

110. S. Serlio, *The Second Book of Architecture,* English Translation, London, 1611.

111. B. no. 8, p. 41.

112. V. 6. 3 and 8.

113. B. no. 8, p. 57.

114. See Gordon Craig, *Books and Theatres,* London and Toronto, 1925, plates 1 and 31.

115. B. no. 45, pp. 63, 66. Unfortunately this is not included in the recent publication by P. Simpson and C. F. Bell, *Designs of Inigo Jones,* Oxford, 1924.

116. In his address " To the Reader."

117. B. Jonson, *Works,* London, 1888, III. 37.

118. From a contemporary account by Philip Stringer; see J. Nichols, *Progresses, etc. of King James the First,* London, 1828, I. 530 ff.

119. B. Jonson, *Works,* London, 1888, III. 60.

120. *History and Antiquities of the Colleges and Halls in the University of Oxford,* Oxford, 1792–6, II. 407 ff.

121. For the former see B. no. 90, p. 185; for the latter, B. no. 44.

122. B. no. 90, p. 187.

123. John Higins, *Nomenclator* (1584), s. v. *machina.* I am indebted for this citation to Campbell (B. no. 8), p. 133.

124. B. no. 50, Second series, p. 115.

125. Canto XXXII. 80: " Quale al cader delle cortine suole " etc. The translation is my own.

126. *Works,* London, 1888, III. 3.

127. Quoted by Lawrence (B. no. 50), Second series, p. 118.

128. In recent years the Greek theatre has begun again to exert a powerful influence which is manifesting itself, first, in the construction of open-air theatres more or less resembling the ancient types, second, in the simplification of the seating arrangements of indoor theatres. These two significant movements are admirably described by Cheney (B. no. 15) and by H. K. Moderwell, *The Theatre of Today,* New York, 1923, chap. XIV.; see also B. no. 61.

Of the " Greek " theatres in America that at Point Loma, near San Diego, California, most nearly resembles the theatre of the days of Aeschylus. The others are more Roman or Graeco-Roman than Greek, though none is strictly true to type. The most noteworthy are those at (1) The University of California, Berkeley; (2) Pomona College, Claremont, California; (3) Occidental College, Los Angeles, California; (4) Hollywood, Los Angeles (the so-called "Hollywood Bowl"); (5) Bakersfield, California; and (6) "Cranbrook," near Detroit, Michigan.

129. D. Rossetti, *Petrarca, Giule Celso e Boccaccio,* Trieste, 1828, p. 324.

130. B. no. 84, pp. 89 ff.

131. B. no. 60, p. 59.

132. Of especial interest at this time (Dec. 1926) is the performance of the *Prometheus Bound* of Aeschylus, to be held on May 9 and 10 in the ancient theatre at Delphi, Greece, under the direction of Mr. and Mrs. Angelo Sikelianos of Athens. The preparations for this Delphic Festival have been in progress since the year 1924.

133. B. no. 88, vol. I, p. 135.

134. E. Dickinson, *The Study of the History of Music,* New York, 1921, p. 67.

BIBLIOGRAPHY

A complete bibliography of the subject treated in the foregoing pages would fill a sizable volume. In the following selection the list has been pared to the quick; for other titles see the preceding notes and consult the bibliographies contained in the books mentioned below, especially those numbered 1, 2, 5, 8, 26, 31, 91 and 94. Many useful articles will be found in Pauly-Wissowa, *Real-encyclopädie d. class. Altertumswissenschaft,* and in Daremberg et Saglio, *Dictionnaire des antiquités grecques et romaines.*

1. ADAMS, J. Q., *Shakespearean Playhouses.* Boston, 1917.
2. ALLEN, J. T., *The Greek Theatre of the Fifth Century Before Christ.* Berkeley, 1919.
3. BETHE, E., *Prolegomena zur Geschichte des Theaters im Alterthum.* Leipzig, 1896.
4. BIEBER, M., "Die Herkunft des tragischen Kostüms," in *Jahrb. d. k. d. arch. Inst.,* XXXII. 15 ff. (1917).
5. ——, *Die Denkmäler zum Theaterwesen im Altertum.* Berlin, 1920.
6. BUTCHER, S. H., *Aristotle's Theory of Poetry and Fine Art.*[4] London, 1911.
7. CAMPBELL, L., *A Guide to Greek Tragedy.* London, 1891.
8. CAMPBELL, L. B., *Scenes and Machines on the English Stage during the Renaissance.* Cambridge, 1923.
9. CAPPS, E., " The Greek Stage According to the Extant

Dramas," in *Trans. Amer. Phil. Assoc.*, XXII. 1 ff. (1891).

10. ——, "The Chorus in Later Greek Drama with Reference to the Stage Question," in *Papers of the Amer. School at Athens*, VI. 392 ff. (1897).

11. ——, "The Introduction of Comedy into the City Dionysia," in *Dec. Publ. of the Univ. of Chicago*, VI. 259 ff. (1904).

12. CHAMBERS, E. K., *The Mediaeval Stage*. 2 vols. Oxford, 1903.

13. ——, *The Elizabethan Stage*. 4 vols. Oxford, 1923.

14. CHASSANG, A., *Des essais dramatiques imités de l'antiquité au XIVe et au XVe siecle*. Paris, 1852.

15. CHENEY, S., *The Open-air Theatre*. New York, 1918.

16. CORNFORD, F. M., *The Origin of Attic Comedy*. London, 1914.

17. CREIZENACH, W. M. A., *Geschichte des neueren Dramas*. 5 vols. Halle a S., 1893–1916.

18. CUNLIFFE, J. W., *The Influence of Seneca on Elizabethan Tragedy*. London, 1893.

19. ——, *Early English Classical Traditions*. Oxford, 1912.

20. DIETERICH, A., *Pulcinella, pompejanische Wandbilder und römische Satyrspiele*. Leipzig, 1897.

21. DÖRPFELD, W., und REISCH, E., *Das griechische Theater*. Athens, 1896.

22. DÖRPFELD, W., "Das Theater von Priene und die griechische Bühne," in *Athenische Mitteilungen*, XLIX. 50 ff. (1924).

23. DUFF, J. W., *A Literary History of Rome from the Origins to the Close of the Golden Age.*[2] London, 1910.

24. FERRARI, G., *La Scenografia*. Milan, 1902.

25. FIECHTER, E. R., *Die baugeschichtliche Entwicklung des antiken Theaters*. München, 1914.

26. FLICKINGER, R. C., *The Greek Theater and its Drama.*[3] Chicago, 1926.

27. FOWLER, W. W., *Roman Festivals of the Period of the Republic*. London, 1901.

BIBLIOGRAPHY

28. ——, *Social Life at Rome in the Age of Cicero*. London, 1901.

29. FRICKENHAUS, A., " Zum Ursprung von Satyrspiel und Tragödie," in *Jahrb. d. k. d. arch. Inst.* XXXII. 1 ff. (1917).

30. ——, *Die altgriechische Bühne*. Strassburg, 1917.

31. FRIEDLÄNDER, L., *Darstellungen aus der Sittengeschichte Roms in der Zeit von August bis zum Ausgang der Antonine*.[9] Zweiter Teil. Leipzig, 1920. Seventh Edition translated by Freese, J. H., and Magnus, L. A., and Gough, A. B.: *Roman Life and Manners under the Early Empire*. London and New York, 1908–1913.

32. GEFFCKEN, J., *Die griechische Tragödie*. Leipzig, 1918.

33. GERKAN, A. VON, *Das Theater von Priene*. München, 1921.

34. GOODELL, T. D., *Athenian Tragedy*. New Haven, 1920.

35. GRAY, J. H., " Roman Public Games " and " The Roman Theatre," in Sandys, J. E., *Companion to Latin Studies*,[3] pp. 503 ff. Cambridge, England, 1921.

36. HAIGH, A. E., *The Tragic Drama of the Greeks*. Oxford, 1896.

37. ——, *The Attic Theatre*.[3] Edited by Pickard-Cambridge, A. W., Oxford, 1907.

38. HAINS, D. D., " Greek Plays in America," in *The Classical Journal*, VI. 24 ff. (1910).

39. HEINEMANN, K., *Die tragischen Gestalten der Griechen in der Weltliteratur*. 2 vols. Leipzig, 1920.

40. HENSE, O., *Die Modificirung der Maske in der griechischen Tragödie*.[2] Frieburg im B., 1905.

41. INAMA, V., *Il Teatro Antico Greco e Romano*. Milan, 1910.

42. JEVONS, F. B., " Masks and the Origin of Greek Drama," in *Folklore*, XXVII. 171 ff. (1916).

43. KENT, R. G., " The Time Element in the Greek Drama," in *Trans. Am. Phil. Assoc.*, XXXVII. 39 ff. (1906).

44. KEITH, W. G., " Designs for the First Movable Scenery on the English Stage," in *Burlington Magazine*, XXV. 29 ff., 85 ff. (1914).

[195]

BIBLIOGRAPHY

45. ——, "A Theatre Project of Inigo Jones," in *Ibid.*, XXXI. 61 ff., 105 ff. (1917).

46. KLEIN, F., "Der Chor in den wichtigsten Tragödien der französischen Renaissance," in *Münchener Beitr. z. romanischen u. englischen Philologie*, XII. (1897).

47. KNAPP, C., "The Roman Theater," in *Art and Archaeology*, I. 137 ff., 187 ff. (1915).

48. LANCASTER, H. C., "A Neglected Passage on the Three Unities of French Classical Drama," in *Publ. Mod. Lang. Assoc.* XXIII. 307 ff. (1908).

49. LAW, H. H., *Studies in the Songs of Plautine Comedy.* Menasha, Wisconsin, 1902.

50. LAWRENCE, W. J., *The Elizabethan Playhouse and Other Studies.* Stratford-upon-Avon, 1912. Second Series, 1913.

51. LEGRAND, P. E., *Daos, Tableau de la comédie grecque pendant la période dite nouvelle.* Lyon, 1910. Transl. by James Loeb: *The New Greek Comedy.* London and New York, 1917.

52. LEO, F., *Plautinische Forschungen.*[2] Berlin, 1912.

53. ——, *Geschichte der römischen Literatur.* Erster Band: *Die archaische Literatur.* Berlin, 1913.

54. LORD, L. E., *Aristophanes, His Plays and His Influence,* in the Series "Our Debt to Greece and Rome." New York, 1923.

55. LUCAS, F. L., *Seneca and Elizabethan Tragedy.* Cambridge, 1922.

56. ——, *Euripides and His Influence,* in the Series "Our Debt to Greece and Rome." New York, 1923.

57. MANTZIUS, K., *A History of Theatrical Art in Ancient and Modern Times.* Translation by L. von Cossel. 6 vols. London, 1902–1921.

58. MATTHEWS, B., *The Development of the Drama.* New York, 1903.

59. ——, *A Study of the Drama.* New York, 1910.

60. ——, *A Book About the Theater.* New York, 1916.

61. MORITZ, E., *Das antike Theater und die modernen Reformbestrebungen im Theaterbau.* Berlin, 1910.

BIBLIOGRAPHY

62. MOULTON, R. G., *The Ancient Classical Drama*. Oxford, 1898.
63. MÜLLER, ALBERT, *Lehrbuch der griechischen Bühnenalterthümer*. Freiburg im B., 1886.
64. MÜLLER, ADOLF, *Die Griechische Drama und seine Wirkungen bis zum Gegenwart*. Sammlung-Kösel, München, 1908.
65. NAVARRE, O., *Le Théâtre grec*. Paris, 1925.
66. NORWOOD, G., *Greek Tragedy*. London, 1920.
67. O'CONNOR, J. B., *Chapters in the History of Actors and Acting in Ancient Greece*. Chicago, 1908.
68. PUCHSTEIN, O., *Die griechische Bühne*. Berlin, 1901.
69. REES, K., *The So-called Rule of Three Actors in the Classical Greek Drama*. Chicago, 1908.
70. ——, "The Significance of the Parodoi in the Greek Theater," in *The Amer. Journ. Phil.*, XXXII. 377 ff. (1911).
71. ——, "The Function of the Prothyron in the Production of Greek Plays," in *Class. Phil.*, X. 117 ff. (1915).
72. REICH, H., *Der Mimus*. 2 vols. Berlin, 1903.
73. RIDGEWAY, W., *The Origin of Tragedy*. Cambridge, England, 1910.
74. RIBBECK, O., *Die römische Tragödie in Zeitalter der Republik*. Leipzig, 1875.
75. ROBERT, K., *Die Masken der neueren attischen Komödie*. Halle a S., 1911.
76. ROBINSON, D. M., "Greek Drama," in J. Hastings' *Encyclopaedia of Religion and Ethics*, New York, Vol. IV. 879 ff., 1912.
77. SAUNDERS, C., *Costume in Roman Comedy*. New York, 1909.
78. ——, "The Introduction of Masks on the Roman Stage," in *The Amer. Journ. Phil.*, XXXII. 58 ff. (1911).
79. SCHANZ, M., *Geschichte der römischen Litteratur*. 7 vols. Various editions. München, 1907–1920.
80. SELLAR, Y. W., *Roman Poets of the Republic*.[3] Oxford, 1889.

BIBLIOGRAPHY

81. SITTL, K., *Die Gebärden der Griechen und Römer*. Leipzig, 1890.

82. SMITH, K. F., "Roman Drama," in J. Hastings' *Encyclopaedia of Religion and Ethics*, New York, Vol. IV, 898 ff., 1912.

83. SMITH, K. K., "The Use of the High-soled Shoe or Buskin in Greek Tragedy," in *Harv. Stud. in Class. Phil.*, XVI. 123 ff. (1905).

84. SPINGARN, J. E., *A History of Literary Criticism in the Renaissance*.² New York, 1908.

85. STRATTON, C., "Greek Influence upon the Stage," in *Art and Archaeology*, III. 251 ff. (1916).

86. STUART, D. C., "The Origin of Greek Tragedy," in *Trans. Amer. Phil. Assoc.*, XLVII. 173 ff. (1916).

87. ——, "Stage Decoration and Unity of Place in France in the Seventeenth Century," in *Modern Philology*, X. 393 ff. (1912–1913).

88. SYMONDS, J. A., *The Renaissance in Italy*. Part IV: *Italian Literature*. 2 vols. New York, 1882.

89. TEUFFEL, W. S., *Geschichte der römischen Literatur*.⁶ 3 vols. Leipzig, 1910–1916.

90. THORNDIKE, A. H., *Shakespeare's Theater*. New York, 1916.

91. VAN HOOK, LA RUE, *Greek Life and Thought*. New York, 1923.

92. VITRUVIUS, *The Ten Books on Architecture*, translated by M. H. Morgan. Cambridge, Mass., 1914.

93. WARNECKE, B., "Die Vortragskunst der römischen Schauspieler," in *Neue Jahrb. f. d. klass. Altertum.*, XXI. 704 ff. (1908).

94. ——, "Gebärdenspiel und Mimik der römischen Schauspieler," in *Ibid.*, XXV. 580 ff. (1910).

95. WHITE, J. W., "The Stage in Aristophanes," in *Harv. Stud. in Class. Phil.*, II. 159 ff. (1891).

96. ——, *The Verse of Greek Comedy*. London, 1912.

INDEX

INDEX

ACCIUS, 124; *Clytemnestra*, 19, 130

Acting (style of), 146–148, 197 f.

Actor, 58

Actors, 26, 131–148, 197; contests of, 33, 43, 132; guilds of, 49, 132 f.; number of, 14, 15, 132, 135–139; solos, 120 ff.; status of, 58, 133–135; troupes, 49, 136

Acts (number of), 125, 168–170, 173 f.

Admission (price of), 39

Aeschylus, 15, 39, 40, 45, 69, 72, 76, 110, 112, 116; *Agamemnon*, 75, 105, 128, 130, 182; *Choephori*, 75; *Eumenides*, 75, 108, 126, 129, 130; *Oedipodeia*, 39; *Persians*, 88, 104; *Seven against Thebes*, 39, 122, 128; *Prometheus Bound*, 192; *Suppliants*, 104, 128, 137; *Women of Aetna*, 88

Aesopus, 134

Agatharchus, 75, 151

Agathon, 111, 124

Agon, 122

Agonothetes, 46

Altar(s), 63, 74, 86, 101

Angiportum, 106

Architecton, 40

Arion, 12, 13

Aristophanes, 9, 69, 112, 123, 137, 166, 172, 180, 198; *Acharnians*, 110, 179; *Birds*, 105, 137, 181; *Clouds*, 105, 113, 116; *Ecclesiazusae*, 107, 126; *Frogs*, 40, 103, 107; *Lysistrata*, 140; *Peace*, 115; *Plutus*, 107; *Thesmophoriazusae*, 111; *Wasps*, 105, 181

Aristotle, 12, 75, 150, 168, 169, 179

Artists of Dionysus, 49, 132

Atellanae. See Fabulae

Audience, 39, 59, 60, 109

Auditorium, 62–64, 81, 90, 93, 95, 156

Aulaeum. See Curtain

BATHYLLUS, 27

CANTICA, 27, 28, 123

Cavea, 91, 92, 94, 96

Changes (of set, etc.), 107, 108, 126

Charonian steps, 115

Choregus (choregia), 43 ff., 58

Chorus, 26, 27, 37, 118–128, 168, 177–179, 180, 181

Clarinet, 7, 38, 123, 185

Comedy: Greek, 4, 7, 8, 124;

[201]

INDEX

Old, 9, 32, 33, 122, 139–141, 181; Middle, 9 f.; New, 9, 41, 81, 118, 124, 141, 142, 166; Roman, 18, 20; Renaissance, 180 f.; Modern, 167 ff., 180 f.

Comus, 7, 32, 35, 139

Contests: of actors, 33, 43, 45, 132; of choregi, 43; of dithyrambic choruses, 35, 37; of plays, 35, 38; of poets, 43; at Rome, 59

Coryphaeus, 127, 131, 135

Costumes, 11, 26, 28, 45, 46, 139–146, 197

Cothorni, 144–146, 198

Crane, 115

Curtain, 108, 109, 164, 165

Dance(s), 26, 28, 119, 122, 123, 127

Deus ex machina, 117, 163, 176

Deuteragonist, 138–139

Diazoma(ta), 65, 91, 93, 94

Didascalia, 39

Didascalos, 45

Dionysia: City, 34–38, 40–47, 57, 70, 89; Rural, 48, 49; see Lenaea

Dionysus, 30–32, 34, 36, 50, 57, 70, 71, 87, 144, 190

Dithyramb, 10, 12, 13, 33, 35, 38, 45

Dominus, 58

Door(s), 84, 90, 92, 105, 106, 155, 157

Drama: ancient, 1–29, 118 ff.; mediaeval, 29, 60, 149, 150, 152, 174, 177; neo-classical and modern, 150, 168, 171, 179–181; see also Comedy, Tragedy, etc.

Eccyclema, 111–112, 115

Embolima. See Interludes

Emmeleia, 119

Ennius, 124, 130

Entrances. See Parodi

Epicharmus, 6

Epilogues, 174–177

Episkenion, 67, 83

Euripides, 15, 16, 39, 42, 69, 112, 116, 120, 124, 125, 168, 173, 175, 176, 177, 179; *Alcestis*, 105, 126; *Andromache*, 105, 135; *Andromeda*, 104; *Bellerophon*, 116; *Cyclops*, 12, 105; *Helena*, 102, 103; *Ion*, 102, 103; *Iphigenia Taurica*, 179; *Orestes*, 113, 136; *Phoenissae*, 175; *Rhesus*, 103, 126

Exodia, 24, 25

Exostra, 111

Expenses of festivals, 44, 45, 49, 57

Fabulae: Atellanae, 21, 23, 24, 56, 134, 149; palliatae, 20, 143; praetextae, 19, 56, 143, 186; togatae, 20, 56, 143

Festivals, 30 ff.; 50 ff.

Flats, 108, 109, cf. 162, 163

Gesture, 28, 147, 186, 198

Grex, 58

[202]

INDEX

INDEX

Our Debt to Greece and Rome

AUTHORS AND TITLES

AUTHORS AND TITLES

AESCHYLUS AND SOPHOCLES. *J. T. Sheppard.*

GREEK RELIGION. *Walter Woodburn Hyde.*

SURVIVALS OF ROMAN RELIGION. *Gordon J. Laing.*

MYTHOLOGY. *Jane Ellen Harrison.*

ANCIENT BELIEFS IN THE IMMORTALITY OF THE SOUL. *Clifford H. Moore.*

STAGE ANTIQUITIES. *James Turney Allen.*

PLAUTUS AND TERENCE. *Gilbert Norwood.*

ROMAN POLITICS. *Frank Frost Abbott.*

PSYCHOLOGY, ANCIENT AND MODERN. *G. S. Brett.*

ANCIENT AND MODERN ROME. *Rodolfo Lanciani.*

WARFARE BY LAND AND SEA. *Eugene S. McCartney.*

THE GREEK FATHERS. *James Marshall Campbell.*

GREEK BIOLOGY AND MEDICINE. *Henry Osborn Taylor.*

MATHEMATICS. *David Eugene Smith.*

LOVE OF NATURE AMONG THE GREEKS AND ROMANS. *H. R. Fairclough.*

ANCIENT WRITING AND ITS INFLUENCE. *B. L. Ullman.*

GREEK ART. *Arthur Fairbanks.*

ARCHITECTURE. *Alfred M. Brooks.*

ENGINEERING. *Alexander P. Gest.*

MODERN TRAITS IN OLD GREEK LIFE. *Charles Burton Gulick.*

ROMAN PRIVATE LIFE. *Walton Brooks McDaniel.*

GREEK AND ROMAN FOLKLORE. *William Reginald Halliday.*

ANCIENT EDUCATION. *J. F. Dobson.*